Music Composition 2

JONATHAN E. PETERS

Copyright © 2014 Jonathan E. Peters

All rights reserved.

ISBN-10: 1503284611
ISBN-13: 978-1503284616

TO MY PARENTS…

…for the gift of life and for paying for all those music lessons!

CONTENTS

1	Tonal Function	Pg. 1
2	Diatonic Chord Substitution	Pg. 18
3	Developing Harmonic Progressions	Pg. 32
4	The Harmonic Phrase	Pg. 43
5	The Harmonic Period	Pg. 50
6	Chromatic Chord Substitution	Pg. 59
7	Modulation	Pg. 72
8	Harmonic Rhythm	Pg. 83
9	Musical Texture	Pg. 91
10	Binary Form	Pg. 105
11	Ternary Form	Pg. 119
12	Rondo & Arch Forms	Pg. 128
13	Strophic & Variation Forms	Pg. 136
14	Sonata Form	Pg. 142

1. TONAL FUNCTION

BEFORE WE BEGIN

This is the second course in a two course series on music composition. The first course, *Music Composition 1*, dealt with the study of rhythmic and melodic composition. If you have not taken *Music Composition 1*, it is highly recommended that you do so before taking *Music Composition 2*. *Music Composition 2* is divided into two portions. The first portion deals with the study of harmonic composition. The second portion deals with the study of compositional form.

To get free life-time access to all of the audio samples for the diagrams in this book and also quizzes for each lesson, please go to:

https://www.udemy.com/musiccomposition2companion

Click on, "Enter Password" and enter **3b78fj4**

Click on, "Start Learning Now".

The next window will ask you to sign up for a Udemy account (if you do not have one already). Enter your name, e-mail address, and create a password for your account.

That's it!

CHORDS OF THE SCALE

If you have studied music theory then you know that music written in a "key" is built upon the notes of the scale. The notes of the scale are the palette of pitches a composer can choose from to form a melody. They are also the notes the composer can use to form harmonies.

Using only the notes of the "C major" scale we can form the following chords.

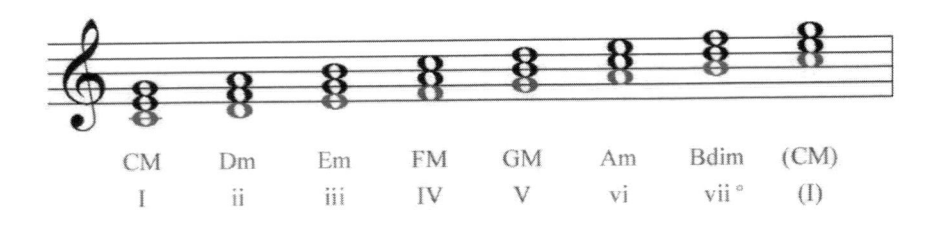

CM	Dm	Em	FM	GM	Am	Bdim	(CM)
I	ii	iii	IV	V	vi	vii°	(I)

If a composer is writing a piece in the key of "C major", these seven chords are the chords they will most likely use to harmonize their melodies and to construct their chords.

Note: It is possible for a chord to use pitches outside of the key, but right now we are only dealing with diatonic chords (chords that use only the pitches of the diatonic scale).

In this lesson we will look at three chords in particular: I, IV, and V. These chords are called the primary chords. It doesn't matter which notes of the scale we choose to form our melodies, they can all be harmonized with one of these three chords. The following diagram will help to illustrate this. The right hand consists of a "C major" scale. The left hand consists only of primary chords and harmonizes the scale.

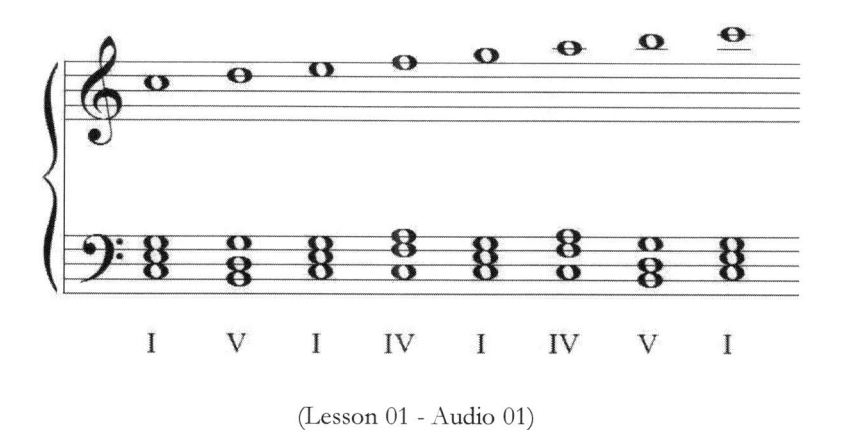

(Lesson 01 - Audio 01)

DEPARTURE, ANTICIPATION & RETURN

When chords move from one to another in succession toward a definite tonal goal it is called a **chord progression**. Many chord progressions conform to the basic structure of "departure, anticipation, and return". "Departure" is the moving away from the tonic, "anticipation" is the aural expectation of hearing the tonic again, and "return" is the coming back home to the tonic chord. (The tonic chord is the "I" chord or root chord of the key. It is the chord in which we feel at rest.) To achieve this structure of "departure, anticipation and return", at least three different chords are needed; the tonic chord and two other chords.

The first thing needed is to establish a tonic. A single chord by itself cannot establish a tonic since a single chord is ambiguous and could be interpreted in a number of ways.

The "F major chord" in the preceding diagram could be any of the following.

- "I" chord (in the key of "F major")
- "V" chord (in the key of "B flat major")
- "IV" chord (in the key of "C major")
- "VI" chord (in the key of "A minor")

If a single chord cannot establish a tonic, can a progression made up of only two chords establish a tonic? The answer is…not really. A progression of only two chords is still not enough to establish a tonic since there continues to be some degree of ambiguity as to which chord is acting as the tonic. Take for example the following chord progression.

TONAL FUNCTION

(Lesson 01 - Audio 02)

It sounds like we might be in the key of "F major" and that the progression is a "V" (C major chord) moving to a "I" (F major chord). The problem is, without more musical context we really can't tell if we are coming or going. In other words, is the second chord the departure from the first chord, or is the first chord the anticipation of the return to the second chord? We therefore need at least three chords to establish a tonic.

Here is the preceding example with more musical context. What at first sounded as if it was in the key of "F major", is actually in the key of "C major".

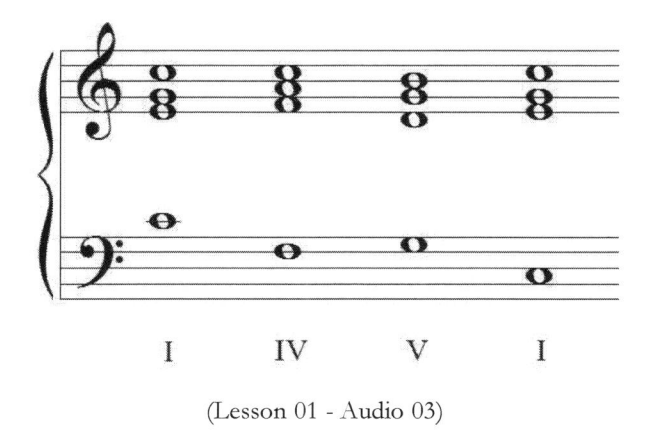

I   IV   V   I

(Lesson 01 - Audio 03)

"IV" serves as the departure from the tonic, "V" sets up the anticipation of the return to the tonic, and "I" is the return to the tonic. As you can see, not only can the primary chords harmonize any melody made up from the pitches of the scale, they also provide the sense of harmonic movement necessary to chord progressions. This brings us to the topic of **tonal function**.

Every chord has a tonal function. Tonal function is the "role" each chord plays in a chord progression. A chord's tonal function is determined by the degree of the scale the chord is built upon. There are three tonal functions: the **tonic function**, the **pre-dominant function** (also called the subdominant function), and the **dominant function**.

- The function of the tonic is to establish the key.
- The function of the pre-dominant is to lead to the dominant.
- The function of the dominant is to lead back to the tonic.

Each of the primary chords falls into one of these categories. The "I" chord obviously has a tonic function, the "IV" chord has a pre-dominant function, and the "V" chord has a dominant function.

Note: This is not to say that every chord progression must follow the pattern: I - IV - V - I. Since this is a beginning course on music composition, knowledge of the three basic tonal functions will serve as a great foundation and springboard for further study.

When a piece is written in a minor key, the primary chords ("i", "iv" and "V") have the same tonal functions as the primary chords in major keys. The "V" chord in the following example is major since we are using the pitches of the "harmonic" minor scale. (See *Music Theory* by the author)

TONAL FUNCTION

        i   iv   V   i

(Lesson 01 - Audio 04)

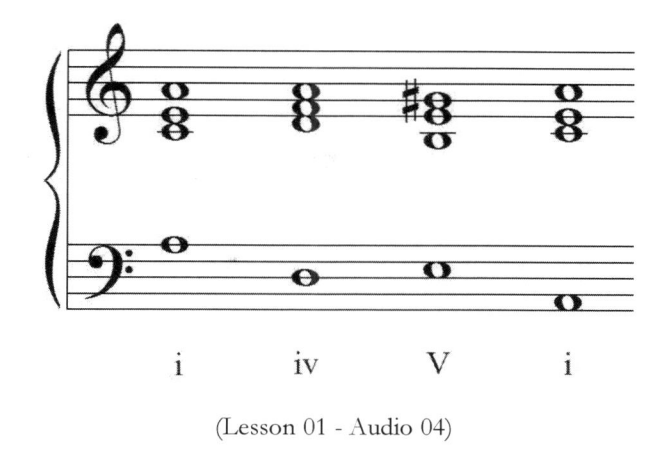

We will learn more about tonal function and other types of chord progressions in the coming lessons.

VOICE LEADING

Since this is a beginning course in music composition we will not be covering more advanced topics such as four-part writing, open and closed voicing, etc. We will however need to understand a few basic principles. One of these principles is the principle of **voice leading**.

Theoretically, any chord can move to any other chord. There are however certain elements that make some chord progressions more appealing than others. One of these elements is the "voice leading" between chords.

The movement from one chord to another is actually at its foundation melodic in nature. To understand this we first have to understand **voice**. Each pitch of a chord is sometimes referred to as a "voice". The top pitch is called the "top voice", the middle pitch is called the "middle voice", and the bottom pitch is called the "bottom voice". Voice leading is the manner in which each voice in one chord transitions to the corresponding voice in the subsequent chord.

If you look at the movement of a "G major" chord in root position to a "C major" chord in root position you will notice that each "voice" moves downwards by a perfect 5th.

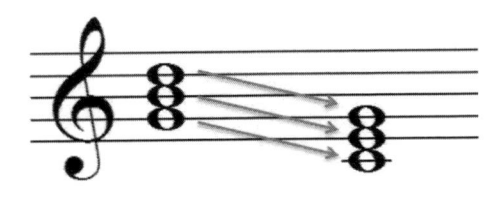

(Lesson 01 - Audio 05)

To create better transitions between chords composers use chord inversions. (See *Music Theory* by the author) This process can be summed up in the principle of voice leading which states: the transition between chords is most pleasant when one (or more) of the voices remains on the same pitch, and one (or more) of the other voices moves by a whole step or half step. Here is the same chord change (a "G major" chord to a "C major" chord) this time using the principle of voice leading.

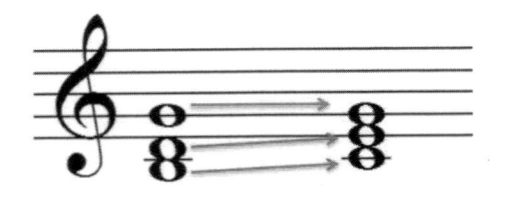

(Lesson 01 - Audio 06)

Why does this work? First of all, by keeping one voice the same in each chord we create continuity between the two chords. Second, movement by steps is the most melodic form of movement. It is both natural to the human voice and the movement that we find present in the scale.

Make sure you understand the principle of voice leading before completing the lesson assignments.

LESSON CONCLUSION

At the end of each lesson in this course you will find four things:

- Memory Questions
- On-line Quiz
- Listening Assignments
- Composition Assignments

Memory questions aid in summarizing and reinforcing the key concepts learned in the lesson. Study them well in order to pass the on-line lesson quiz. The quizzes for each lesson can be found by logging into your course at **www.udemy.com**

After the memory questions and quiz come the listening assignments. Listening to music is an important part of composing. By listening to music written by the masters you will hear ways in which other composers have used the elements of music to create great works of beauty. You may also get inspiration for writing your own compositions. There are a number of ways to find recordings of the assigned pieces.

1) Obtain a subscription to **www.naxos.com**. With a Naxos subscription you get unlimited listening access to their superb CD library. Although you will not own the music, it will be much cheaper than buying all the music assigned with this course.

2) Check your local library for recordings. Your library may also subscribe to **www.freegalmusic.com**. If they do, you can download a specific amount of music each week for free and its yours to keep.

3) Check on-line sources such as **www.musopen.org**.

4) Download MP3 recordings from i-tunes or purchase CDs from amazon.

And finally, at the very end of each lesson you will find the composition assignments. These are to be completed with the free notation software "NotePad". (If you already own notation software you may use that instead.) If you have not already done so, please download and install NotePad on your computer before moving forward. When you open the program for the first time it will ask you to register. In order to get the free tech support for the program you must register.

Download NotePad at: **www.finalemusic.com/NotePad**

The following are the four steps you will take when setting up a document for your assignments.

Step 1: Open NotePad (the Document Setup Wizard screen will appear).

Step 2: Under "Title" enter the assignment name (for example "Lesson 1 Assignment 1"), and under "Composer" enter your full name. Then click "next".

Step 3: In the first column on the left, click on "keyboard". In the second column, click on "piano". Click "add", then click "next".

Step 4: This is where you select the time signature and key signature for your assignment. (NotePad does not allow you to change meter and key within a song.) Leave the number of measures set to the default unless your assignment specifies a number. You can always add or delete measure at any later time.

You should now see a sheet of music paper on the screen with a grand staff (treble and bass clefs) for writing piano music. All the assignments for this course will be written for the piano.

In order to enter notes on to the page we need to make sure that the "Simple Entry Tool" is selected. It should automatically be selected when you start, but in case it ever gets unselected it is the 8th note icon (3rd from the left).

Let's try entering some notes. Click on the quarter note in the note durations bar.

MUSIC COMPOSITION 2

Whenever you press the enter key on your keyboard while this option is selected a quarter note will be entered on the page. Let's press enter four times and enter four quarter notes. You should now see four quarter notes in the first measure. You can also enter notes by clicking with your mouse.

If you want to erase something, simply click on the erase icon.

Once the eraser is selected you can use the arrow keypad on your keyboard to highlight the note you want to erase and then press delete. You can also erase notes by clicking on the note with your mouse.

When you want to hear what you have written use the playback controls.

These are just the basics. Play around with the software for a while and get to know it. There is a help manual and on-line tutorials that can help you with any other questions you might have. And remember, if you register you can get free tech support.

TONAL FUNCTION

If at any point in this course you have music composition questions that you would like answered or if you would like to have each composition assignment reviewed and commented on, please contact the author at his web site **www.ComposerJonathanPeters.com** about receiving these services for a fee.

Remember…how much you get out of this course is determined by how much work you put into it. To gain the most benefit, it is necessary to complete all the quizzes and assignments.

Good luck and happy composing!

Memory Questions

How many distinct chords can be formed using only the pitches of the scale?
Seven distinct chords can be formed using only the pitches of the scale.

What do we call the chords built on the 1st, 4th, and 5th pitches of the scale?
The chords built on the 1st, 4th, and 5th pitches of the scale are called the primary chords.

What is a chord progression?
A chord progression is a succession of chords which move toward a definite tonal goal.

What is the basic chord progression structure?
The basic chord progression structure is "departure, anticipation, and return".

What is tonal function?
Tonal function is the role each chord plays in a chord progression. A chord's tonal function is determined by the degree of the scale the chord is built upon.

What are the three tonal functions?
The three tonal functions are the tonic function, pre-dominant function and dominant function.

What is the function of the tonic?
The function of the tonic is to establish the key.

What is the function of the pre-dominant?
The function of the pre-dominant is to lead to the dominant.

What is the function of the dominant?
The function of the dominant is to lead back to the tonic.

What function does the "I" chord have?
The "I" chord has a tonic function.

What function does the "IV" chord have?
The "IV" chord has a pre-dominant function.

What function does the "V" chord have?
The "V" chord has a dominant function.

What are the individual pitches of a chord referred to as?
The individual pitches of a chord are referred to as voices.

What is voice leading?
Voice leading is the manner in which each voice in one chord transitions to the corresponding voice in the subsequent chord.

What does the principle of voice leading state?
The transition between chords is most pleasant when one (or more) of the voices remains on the same pitch, and one (or more) of the other voices moves by a whole step or half step.

Lesson 1 Quiz

Log in to your course at www.udemy.com and take the quiz for this lesson.

Listening Assignments

Modest Mussorgsky (1839 - 1881)

- Night on Bald Mountain
- Pictures at an Exhibition (listen to the orchestral arrangement by Maurice Ravel)

Nikolai Rimsky-Korsakov (1844 - 1908)

- "Flight of the Bumblebee" from the opera "The Tale of Tsar Saltan"

- Capriccio Espagnol

Composition Assignments

Assignment 1

Log into your course at www.udemy.com. You will find the assignments for this lesson in section 1 under the "Downloadable Materials" tab. Print the .pdf file "**Lesson 01_Assignment 01**". Instructions: One chord is missing from each measure. Using the principle of voice leading learned in this lesson, fill in the missing chords. You will be given the Roman numeral name and the root of the missing chord in the bass. When you are finished, compare your answers with the answer key "**Lesson 01_Assignment 01 Answer Key**" which can also be found under the "Downloadable Materials" tab.

Assignment 2

Log into your course at www.udemy.com. You will find the assignments for this lesson in section 1 under the "Downloadable Materials" tab. Print the .pdf file "**Lesson 01_Assignment 02**". Instructions: Using only "I", "IV" and "V" chords, harmonize the melody "Twinkle, Twinkle, Little Star". Write one chord every two beats and be sure to follow the principle of voice leading. The first chord is given. When you are finished, compare your answers with a possible harmonization in the answer key, **"Lesson 01_Assignment 02 Answer Key"**, which can also be found under the "Downloadable Materials" tab.

Assignment 3

Log into your course at www.udemy.com. You will find the assignments for this lesson in section 1 under the "Downloadable Materials" tab. Print the .pdf file **"Lesson 01_Assignment 03"**. Instructions: Using only "i", "iv" and "V" chords, harmonize the given melody. Write only one chord for each measure and be sure to follow the principle of voice leading. The first chord is given. When you are finished, compare your answers with a possible harmonization in the answer key, **"Lesson 01_Assignment 03 Answer Key"**, which can also be found under the "Downloadable Materials" tab.

2. DIATONIC CHORD SUBSTITUTION

SECONDARY CHORDS

In the last lesson we learned that there are three basic tonal functions: the **tonic function**, the **pre-dominant function**, and the **dominant function**. We saw how each of the primary chords fit into one of these categories. "I" had a tonic function, "IV" had a pre-dominant function, and "V" had a dominant function.

But what about all the other chords that can be built from the pitches of the scale? What function or purpose do they serve? To answer this question let's take a look at the minor chords that can be formed from the pitches of the major scale. The minor chords of the scale are the "vi", "ii" and "iii" chords. (See *Music Theory* by the author) These three chords are called **secondary chords**. (We will use the chords of the "C major" scale for our example.)

DIATONIC CHORD SUBSTITUTION

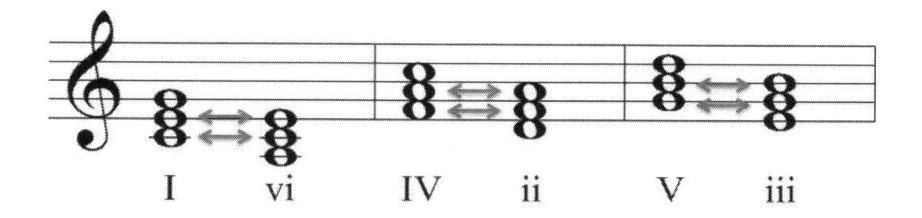

Each of the primary chords in the diagram is followed by a secondary chord. (The secondary chords are basically the relative minor chords.) You will notice that each pair has two notes in common. Because of this fact, the secondary chords are easily interchangeable with their primary counterparts.

When one of the secondary chords is substituted for a primary chord it can take on that primary chord's function. Take for example the "I" chord which has a tonic function. When it is replaced by a "vi" chord, the "vi" chord takes on a tonic function since it is acting "in place of" the tonic. Here is a diagram showing each function, its possible substitution, and their abbreviations.

Tonic (T)	Tonic Substitution (Ts)
I	vi
Pre-dominant (PD)	Pre-dominant Substitution (PDs)
IV	ii
Dominant (D)	Dominant Substitution (Ds)
V	iii

The only chord that we have not dealt with yet is the "vii°" chord. The "vii°" chord is the only chord from the major scale that is diminished. Most music theorists categorize the "vii°" chord as an extension of the "V" chord. Because they share two notes in common, the "vii°" chord can substitute for the "V" chord and take on its dominant function.

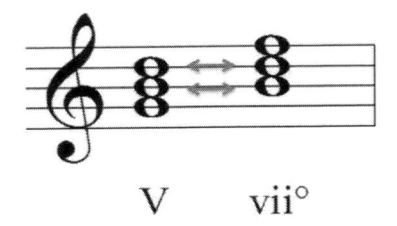

$$V \quad vii°$$

We now have two chords that can act as dominant substitutes - the "iii" chord and the "vii°" chord. This brings us to a problem with the school of thought that says that only the secondary chords can be substitutes for the primary chords. In reality, each chord of the scale actually has two chords that share two notes in common with it; the chord a third above, and the chord a third below. Take for example the "iii" chord in the following diagram.

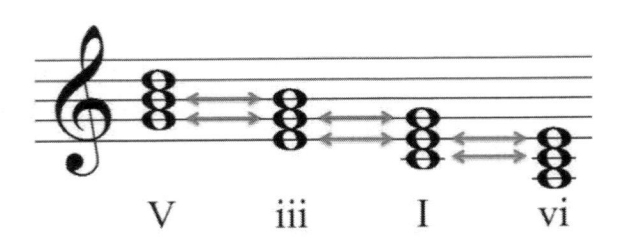

$$V \quad iii \quad I \quad vi$$

As you can see from the diagram, the "iii" chord shares two notes with the "V" chord, but it also shares two notes with the "I" chord. This is why some theorists in the past have argued that the "iii" chord actually has a tonic function rather than a dominant function. Here is a Venn diagram that takes into account both schools of thought.

DIATONIC CHORD SUBSTITUTION

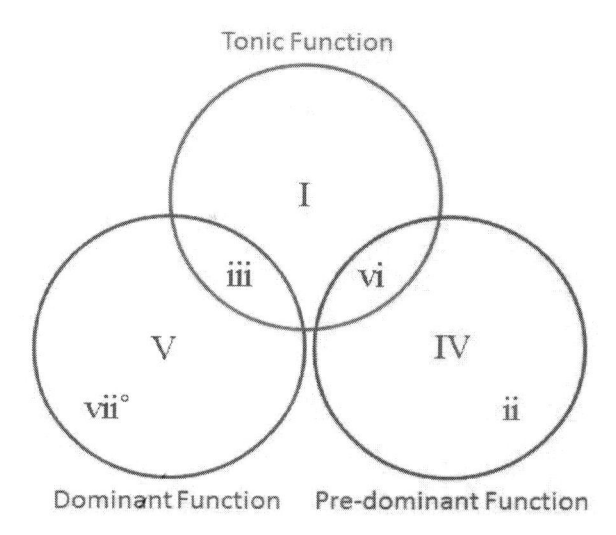

Tonic Function

Dominant Function   Pre-dominant Function

(Venn diagram showing three overlapping circles: Tonic Function contains I with iii and vi in overlaps; Dominant Function contains V with vii° and iii in overlap; Pre-dominant Function contains IV with ii and vi in overlap.)

The primary chords are located in the center of each circle. These chords have only one function. The chords on either side of the primary chords (those a third above and a third below) can have two different functions. For example, the "iii" chord falls into two different circles. It can function as either a tonic or a dominant. The "vi" also falls into two different circles. It can function as either a tonic or a pre-dominant. (The exceptions are the "ii" and "vii°" chords. Although they share two notes in common these chords are not usually substituted for one another.)

You can actually use this Venn diagram to come up with basic chord progressions of your own. Here's how. First of all, you need to remember the basic chord progression structure of "departure, anticipation and return". This structure can be written as the following formula.

$$T - PD - D - T$$

MUSIC COMPOSITION 2

Remember, "T" stands for tonic, "PD" stands for pre-dominant, and "D" stands for dominant. Choose a chord from each circle and then play them in clockwise order beginning and ending with the tonic function circle. Here are some musical examples to illustrate. The first example will use a pre-dominant substitute (PDs).

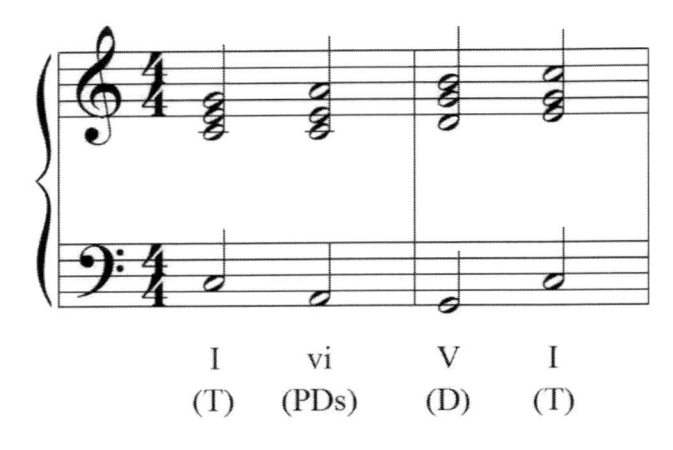

    I   vi   V   I
  (T) (PDs) (D) (T)

(Lesson 02 - Audio 01)

We began with the formula "T - PD - D - T". From the tonic function circle we chose "I" as our starting point. From the pre-dominant function circle we chose the pre-dominant substitution chord "vi". From the dominant function circle we chose the standard "V". Returning to the tonic function circle we chose "I" as our end point.

Here is an example that uses a dominant substitute (Ds) and a tonic substitute (Ts).

DIATONIC CHORD SUBSTITUTION

I	IV	iii	vi
(T)	(PD)	(Ds)	(Ts)

(Lesson 02 - Audio 02)

Once again we began with the formula "T - PD - D - T". From the tonic function circle we chose "I" as our starting point. From the pre-dominant function circle we chose the standard "IV". From the dominant function circle we chose the dominant substitute "iii". Returning to the tonic function circle we chose the tonic substitute "vi" as our end point.

It is important to understand that not every single piece of music ever written fits neatly into this pattern of "T - PD - D - T" (although many do). As a beginning composer, this structure is meant to be a helpful guide and a useful starting point.

Here is a Venn diagram for minor scale chord functions. It works the same way as the previous Venn diagram for the major scale chord functions.

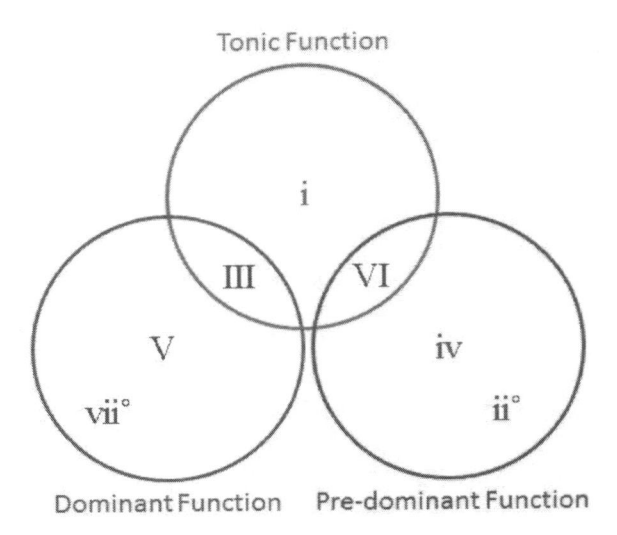

```
                        Tonic Function

                              i

                    III        VI

              V                    iv

         vii°                          ii°

      Dominant Function   Pre-dominant Function
```

Note: Since there are three forms of minor (natural, harmonic, and melodic), certain chords can have more than one possible quality (major, minor or diminished). This diagram shows the most common forms of the chords. ("ii°" and "III" are taken from the natural minor scale; "V" and "vii°" are taken from the harmonic minor scale) Because of this the "III" chord and "V" chord do not share two notes in common but rather only one note in common. They do however still share the dominant function.

Music theorists who have studied centuries' worth of music have found that certain progressions are used more often than others. Here are two charts that illustrate this. The first is for major keys, the second is for minor keys.

DIATONIC CHORD SUBSTITUTION

Starting Chord in Major Key	Most often followed by	Sometimes followed by	Less often followed by
I	IV, V	vi	ii, iii
ii	V, vii°	IV, vi	I, iii
iii	vi	IV	I, ii, V
IV	V, vii°	I, ii	iii, vi
V	I	IV, vi	ii, iii
vi	ii, V	iii, IV	I
vii°	I, iii	vi	ii, IV, V

Starting Chord in Minor Key	Most often followed by	Sometimes followed by	Less often followed by
i	iv, V	VI	ii°, III
ii°	V, vii°	iv, VI	i, III
III	VI	iv	i, ii°, V, vii°
iv	V, vii°	i, ii°	III, VI
V	i	iv, VI	ii°, III
VI	ii°, V, vii°	III, iv	i
vii°	i, III	VI	ii°, iv, V

Note: "ii°" and "III" are taken from the natural minor scale; "V" and "vii°" are taken from the harmonic minor scale.

With so many possible progressions you can see how the formula "T - PD - D - T" is not a strict rule. You don't have to memorize these charts for your lesson quiz, but they may be useful to refer back to as you are writing music for your assignments and if at some point you want to experiment and branch off beyond the "T - PD - D - T" formula.

AMOUNT OF SIMILARITY

In the last lesson we looked at one element that made some chord changes more appealing than others, namely the principle of voice leading. Another element that makes some chord changes more appealing than others is the **amount of similarity** between two chords. The similarity between two chords is determined by how many pitches the two chords have in common with one another. There are three possibilities.

- Triads can have <u>two</u> pitches in common.
- Triads can have <u>one</u> pitch in common.
- Triads can have <u>zero</u> pitches in common.

Triads with two pitches in common create "subtle" chord changes.

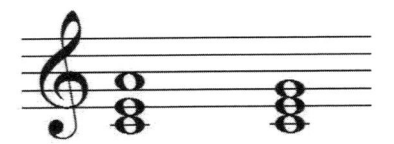

(Lesson 02 - Audio 03)

Triads with one pitch in common create "strong" chord changes.

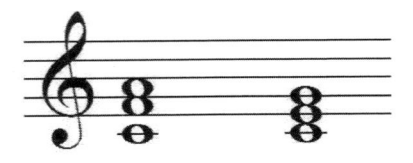

(Lesson 02 - Audio 04)

Triads with zero pitches in common create "stark" chord changes.

DIATONIC CHORD SUBSTITUTION

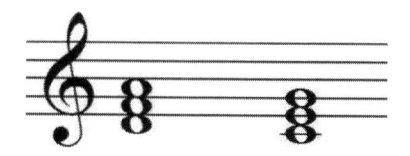

(Lesson 02 - Audio 05)

You should take the three "S's" into consideration when choosing the chords in your progressions. Ask yourself if you want the chord changes to sound **subtle**, **strong** or **stark**.

Note: There are of course other factors to consider such as root strength, position in the harmonic series, and whole step vs. half step movement. Here we are only considering the "amount" of notes in common.

Memory Questions

What do we call the chords built on the 2nd, 3rd, and 6th pitches of the scale?
The chords built on the 2nd, 3rd, and 6th pitches of the scale are called the secondary chords.

Each primary chord has a secondary chord counterpart that shares how many pitches in common?
Each primary chord has a secondary chord counterpart that shares two pitches in common.

What happens when a secondary chord is substituted for a primary chord?
When a secondary chord is substituted for a primary chord it can take on that primary chord's function.

What two functions can the "vi" chord have?
The "vi" chord can have a tonic function or a pre-dominant function.

What two functions can the "iii" chord have?
The "iii" chord can have a tonic function or a dominant function.

What function does the "ii" chord have?
The "ii" chord has a pre-dominant function.

What function does the "vii°" chord have?
The "vii°" has a dominant function.

The basic chord progression structure of "departure, anticipation and return" can be written using what formula?
The basic chord progression structure of "departure, anticipation & return" can be written using the formula "T - PD - D - T".

What does "T - PD - D - T" stand for?
"T - PD - D - T" stands for "tonic - pre-dominant - dominant - tonic".

What do "Ts", "PDs" and "Ds" stand for?
"Ts", "PDs" and "Ds" stand for "tonic substitute", "pre-dominant substitute" and "dominant substitute".

DIATONIC CHORD SUBSTITUTION

Besides voice leading, what is another element that makes some chord changes more appealing than others?
Besides voice leading, another element that makes some chord changes more appealing than others is the amount of similarity between two chords.

How is the similarity between two chords determined?
The similarity between two chords is determined by how many pitches the two chords have in common with one another.

Triads with two pitches in common create what type of chord changes?
Triads with two pitches in common create subtle chord changes.

Triads with one pitch in common create what type of chord changes?
Triads with one pitch in common create strong chord changes.

Triads with zero pitches in common create what type of chord changes?
Triads with zero pitches in common create stark chord changes.

Lesson 2 Quiz

Log in to your course at www.udemy.com and take the quiz for this lesson.

Listening Assignments

Gabriel Fauré (1845 - 1924)

- Requiem in D minor (give special attention to movements IV and VII)

Giacomo Puccini (1858 - 1924)

- The aria "Nessun dorma" from the opera "Turandot"
- The aria "O mio babbino caro" from the opera "Gianni Schicchi
- The duet "O soave fanciulla" from the opera "La Boheme"

Composition Assignments

Assignment 1

Using the <u>first</u> Venn diagram from this lesson, compose a chord progression which conforms to the formula "T - PD - D - T" and notate it with NotePad (or other notation software). You may include a bass line if you wish. Note: The examples in this course have been using the root of each chord in the bass. Although this is not a necessity, it is recommended that as a beginning composer you follow this procedure.

Assignment 2

Using the first Venn diagram from this lesson, compose a different chord progression which conforms to the formula "T - PD - D - T" and notate it with NotePad (or other notation software). You may include a bass line if you wish.

Assignment 3

Using the second Venn diagram from this lesson, compose a chord progression which conforms to the formula "T - PD - D - T" and notate it with NotePad (or other notation software). You may include a bass line if you wish.

Assignment 4

Using the second Venn diagram from this lesson, compose a different chord progression which conforms to the formula "T - PD - D - T" and notate it with NotePad (or other notation software). You may include a bass line if you wish.

Assignment 5

Log into your course at www.udemy.com. You will find the assignments for this lesson in section 2 under the "Downloadable Materials" tab. Print the .pdf file "**Lesson 02_Assignment 05**". Instructions: Using both primary chords and secondary chord substitutes, re-harmonize the melody "Twinkle, Twinkle, Little Star" that you harmonized in lesson 1, assignment 2. The first chord is given.

3. DEVELOPING HARMONIC PROGRESSIONS

EXTENDING FUNCTIONS

In the last lesson we learned about the basic chord progression formula "T - PD - D - T" (Tonic - Pre-dominant - Dominant - Tonic). We also learned how any one of these functions can be replaced by a function substitute (tonic substitute, pre-dominant substitute, and dominant substitute). In this lesson we are going to look at a few ways to develop this basic structure.

One way of developing the basic chord progression structure is through extension. By using a function substitute we can extend any of the three functions. For example, if we wanted to extend the pre-dominant function we could use the "IV" chord followed by one of the pre-dominant substitutes. (Refer back to the Venn diagram in the last lesson for the complete list.) Here is an example.

DEVELOPING HARMONIC PROGRESSIONS

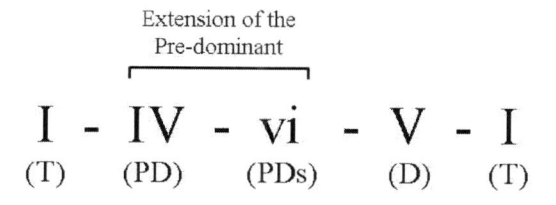

Extension of the
Pre-dominant

I - IV - vi - V - I
(T) (PD) (PDs) (D) (T)

As you can see, the pre-dominant function (IV) has been extended by means of a pre-dominant substitute (vi). This prolongs the progression of moving from the pre-dominant towards the dominant. Listen to what the extension of the pre-dominant sounds like.

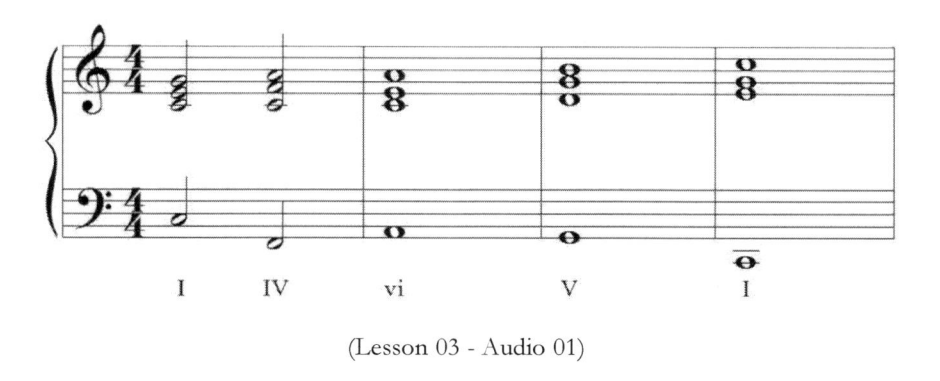

I   IV   vi   V   I

(Lesson 03 - Audio 01)

Here is an example that develops the chord progression by extending the dominant function.

Extension of the
Dominant

I - IV - iii - V - I
(T) (PD) (Ds) (D) (T)

33

As you can see, the dominant function (V) has been extended by means of a dominant substitute (iii). This prolongs the progression of moving from the dominant towards the tonic. Listen to what the extension of the dominant sounds like.

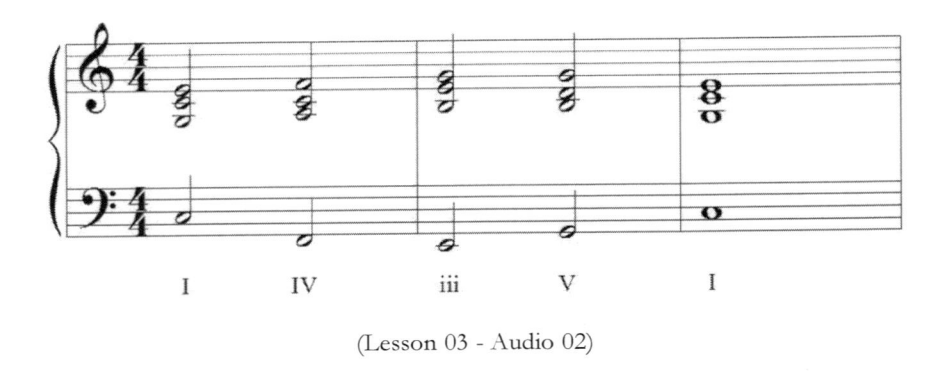

I — IV — iii — V — I

(Lesson 03 - Audio 02)

It is important to note that the function substitute can either precede or follow the normal function. In the first example, the pre-dominant substitute followed the pre-dominant; in the second example, the dominant substitute preceded the dominant.

It is also important to note that more than one function substitute can be used per function.

Extension of the Pre-dominant | Extension of the Dominant

I - vi - IV - ii - V - vii° - I
(T) (PDs) (PD) (PDs) (D) (Ds) (T)

As you can see, three chords function as pre-dominants (one pre-dominant and two pre-dominant substitutes). Listen to how this particular chord progression would sound.

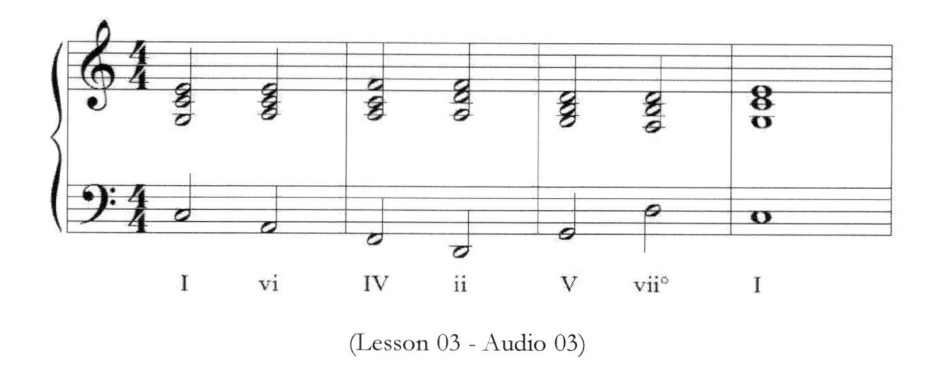

| I | vi | IV | ii | V | vii° | I |

(Lesson 03 - Audio 03)

PROGRESSION CHAINS

Another way composers develop chord progressions is by chaining multiple progressions together to form longer progressions.

I - IV - V - vi - ii - V - I
(T) (PD) (D) (Ts) (PDs) (D) (T)

As you can see, the formula "T - PD - D - T" is used twice. The "vi" chord is a tonic substitute. It serves as the end of the first progression and also the beginning of the second progression. Listen to how this particular chord progression would sound.

MUSIC COMPOSITION 2

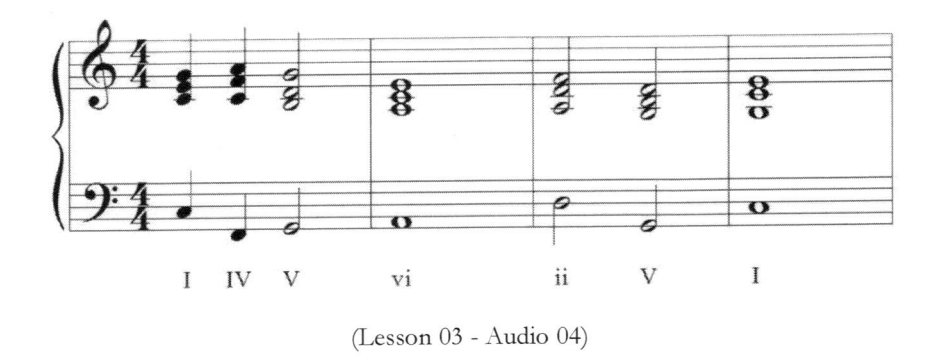

I IV V   vi   ii   V   I

(Lesson 03 - Audio 04)

Although many chord progressions follow the "T - PD - D - T" formula, it is important to re-emphasize that not all progressions do. As a beginning composition student this formula is a great starting point from which you can branch off.

One of the most famous progressions ever composed does not use the "T - PD - D - T" formula. Listen to and analyze the chord progression from Pachelbel's "Canon in D".

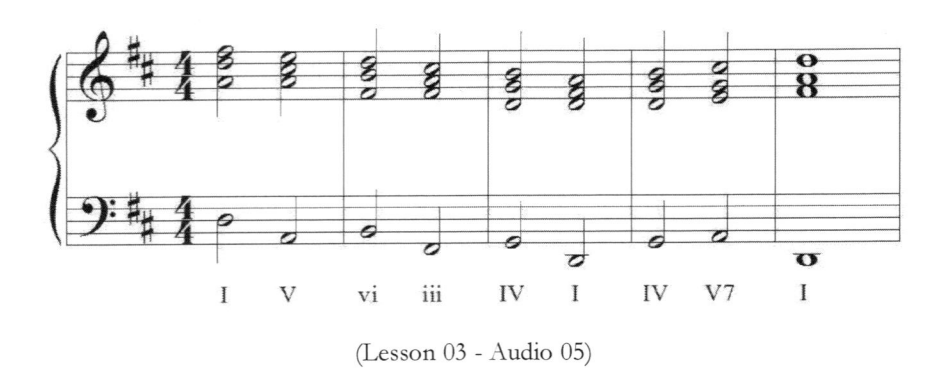

I   V   vi   iii   IV   I   IV   V7   I

(Lesson 03 - Audio 05)

PARTIAL PROGRESSION FORMULA

Another tool used by composers to develop progressions is to break up the basic formula and use portions of it. We can use any portion of the basic formula as long as we retain a tonic. Because of this there are only two possible progressions.

We can leave out the dominant function.

$$I - IV - I$$

Or we can leave out the pre-dominant function.

$$I - V - I$$

Here is an example that combines the last two compositional techniques learned in this lesson (using portions of the basic formula and chaining progressions together).

$$I - IV - I - IV - V - I$$
$$(T) \quad (PD) \quad (T) \quad (PD) \quad (D) \quad (T)$$

Notice how a portion of the formula (T - PD - T) is chained to the complete formula. The "I" chord (tonic function) moves to the "IV" chord (pre-dominant function) but then returns immediately to "I" again. At this point the progression continues using the standard formula "T - PD - D - T". Here is a musical example of the preceding chord progression.

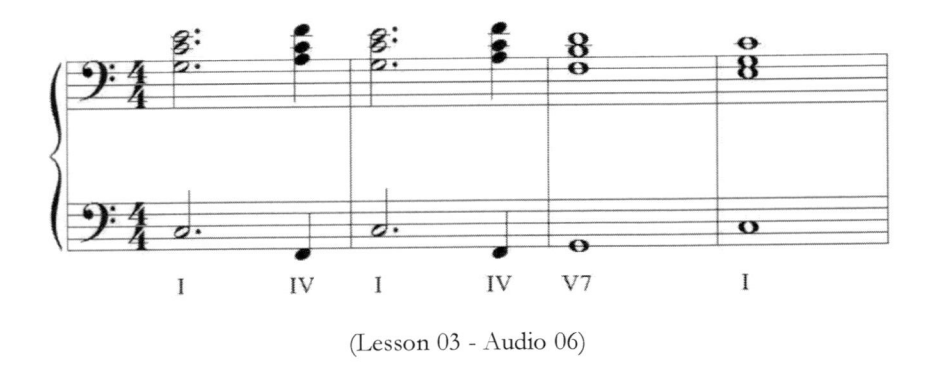

$$\text{I} \quad \text{IV} \quad \text{I} \quad \text{IV} \quad \text{V7} \quad \text{I}$$

(Lesson 03 - Audio 06)

CIRCLE PROGRESSIONS

One popular method of creating chord progressions is through **circle progressions**. Circle progressions are based upon the circle of 5ths. (See *Music Theory* by the author)

If you look at the bass line in the following example you will notice the pattern: "descending perfect 5th" followed by an "ascending perfect 4th" (with the exception of the augmented 4th between "F" and "B"). This is pattern is based upon the circle of 5ths since an ascending perfect 4th is the equivalent of an inverted perfect 5th.

DEVELOPING HARMONIC PROGRESSIONS

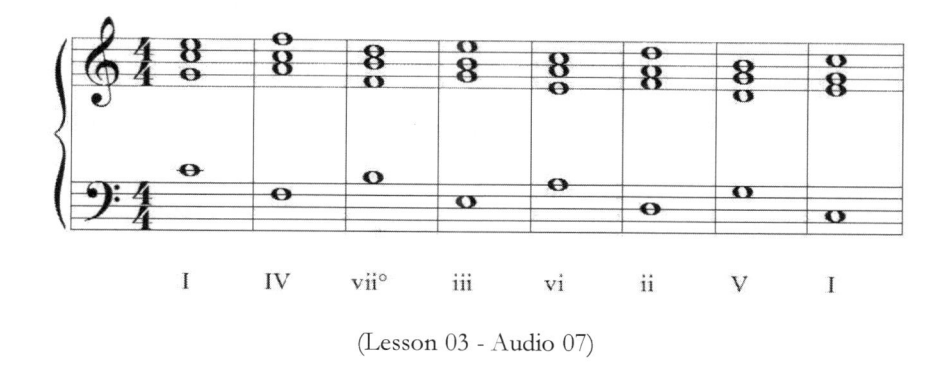

I   IV   vii°   iii   vi   ii   V   I

(Lesson 03 - Audio 07)

Memory Questions

What are some of the ways composers can develop the basic chord progression formula?
Composers can develop the basic chord progression formula by extending functions, chaining progressions together, using portions of the formula, or any combination of these three techniques.

How can we extend a function?
We can extend a function by using a series of chords that share the same function.

How can we chain progressions together?
We can chain progressions together by overlapping the end of one and the start of another.

What portion of the basic chord progression formula can we leave out?
We can leave out either the pre-dominant function or the dominant function.

What is a circle progression?
A circle progression is a chord progression based on the circle of 5ths.

Lesson 3 Quiz

Log in to your course at www.udemy.com and take the quiz for this lesson.

Listening Assignments

Gustav Mahler (1860 - 1911)

- Symphony No. 2 "The Resurrection Symphony"

Composition Assignments

Assignment 1

Compose a chord progression that extends <u>one</u> of the three functions and notate it with NotePad (or other notation software). You may include a bass line if you wish.

Assignment 2

Compose a chord progression that extends <u>two</u> of the three functions and notate it with NotePad (or other notation software). You may include a bass line if you wish.

Assignment 3

Compose a chord progression that extends <u>all</u> three functions and notate it with NotePad (or other notation software). You may include a bass line if you wish.

Assignment 4

Compose a longer chord progression that chains two chord progressions together and notate it with NotePad (or other notation software). Be sure to include function substitutes. You may include a bass line if you wish.

Assignment 5

Compose a chord progression that combines a progression chain and a partial progression (leave out either the pre-dominant or the dominant) and notate it with NotePad (or other notation software). Be sure to include function substitutes. You may include a bass line if you wish.

Assignment 6

Log into your course at www.udemy.com. You will find the assignments for this lesson in section 3 under the "Downloadable

Materials" tab. Print the .pdf file **"Lesson 03_Assignment 06"**. Instructions: Compose a circle progression using the bass line and Roman numerals provided to you. Be sure to follow the principle of voice leading. When you are finished, compare your progression with the progression in the answer key **"Lesson 03_Assignment 06 Answer Key"** which can also be found under the "Downloadable Materials" tab.

4. THE HARMONIC PHRASE

CADENCES

The harmonic phrase is a succession of chords ending in a cadence. A cadence is like musical punctuation. It is defined as a progression of two chords that expresses some degree of finality.

There are four types of cadences: **authentic**, **plagal**, **half** and **deceptive**.

- Authentic cadence ("V" to "I", or "V^7" to "I")
- Plagal cadence ("IV" to "I")
- Half cadence ("I" to "V"; sometimes "ii", "vi", or "IV" is used in place of "I")
- Deceptive cadence ("V" to a chord other than "I", most often it is "V" to "vi")

Each of these cadences has a different strength and helps to determine the types of phrases within a piece of music.

TYPES OF HARMONIC PHRASES

When we studied rhythm and melody in *Music Composition 1* we found that there were three basic types of phrases:

1. Those that suggest continuation
2. Those that suggest a temporary repose
3. Those that suggest finality

These three types of phrases apply to harmony as well. A harmonic phrase is typically 2-4 measures in length and is tied to the rhythmic and melodic phrase.

Let's look at some musical examples that illustrate each type of harmonic phrase. Here is an example of a harmonic phrase that suggests "continuation".

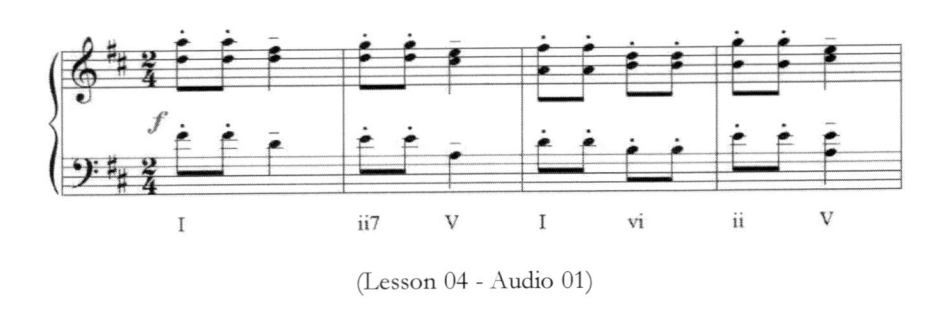

(Lesson 04 - Audio 01)

This piece is in the key of "D major". The last two chords in this example form a half cadence. (Usually a half cadence is "I" to "V", but it can sometimes occur as "ii" to "V" as mentioned previously) Half cadences are weak cadences and suggest a sense of "continuation" because they end on "V". Since "V" is the dominant function and leads back to the tonic, when we hear the final chord in this example our ears demand that the music continue on.

Next, let's look at an example of a harmonic phrase that suggests a "temporary repose".

(musical notation: I - IV - I - IV - I - V - vi)

(Lesson 04 - Audio 02)

This piece is in the key of "F major". The last two chords in this example form a deceptive cadence. Our ears are expecting to hear a "I" after the "V" but instead we get a "vi". If you remember from lesson 2, the "vi" chord can function as a tonic and can therefore be a substitute chord for the "I". A deceptive cadence from "V" to "vi" is a weak cadence and suggests a sense of "temporary repose". When we hear the final chord in this example (the tonic substitute) our ears tell us we are resting "for the moment". We are not fully at rest until we hear the "true" tonic, the "I" chord.

Finally, let's take a look at an example of a harmonic phrase that suggests "finality".

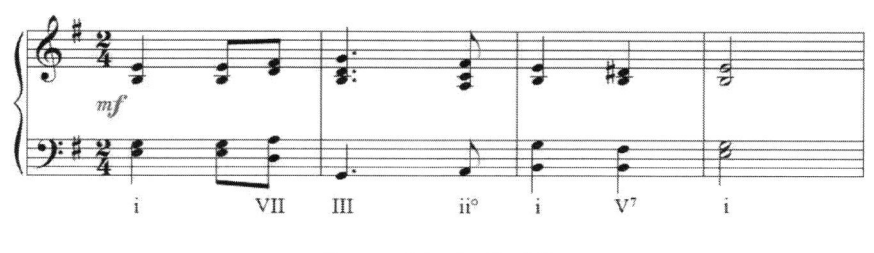

(musical notation: i - VII - III - ii° - i - V⁷ - i)

(Lesson 04 - Audio 03)

This piece is in the key of "E minor". The last two chords in this example form an authentic cadence. Authentic cadences are the strongest type of cadence and suggest "finality". (Plagal cadences are the second strongest cadence.) When our ears hear the final chord we know we are definitely at a stopping point in the music.

Note: Authentic cadences can be more or less "final" sounding depending on whether or not they or "perfect authentic" or "imperfect authentic". (See *Music Theory* by the author)

Along with cadences, another factor that helps determine what a musical phrase suggests is the final chord's tonal function. Here are the basic rules of thumb.

- A musical phrase that ends on any chord with a pre-dominant or dominant function suggests "continuation".
- A musical phrase that ends on a tonic substitute suggests "temporary repose".
- A musical phrase that ends on "I" always suggests "finality".

Memory Questions

What is a cadence?
A cadence is a progression of two chords that expresses some degree of finality.

What is a harmonic phrase?
The harmonic phrase is a succession of chords ending in a cadence.

THE HARMONIC PHRASE

What are the four types of cadences?
The four types of cadences are authentic, plagal, half and deceptive.

What are the three types of harmonic phrases?
The three types of harmonic phrases are those that suggest continuation, those that suggest a temporary repose, and those that suggest finality.

How is continuation suggested?
Continuation is suggested by ending in a half cadence and also by ending on any pre-dominant or dominant function.

How is temporary repose suggested?
Temporary repose is suggested by ending in a deceptive cadence of "V" to "vi" and also by ending on any tonic substitute.

How is finality suggested?
Finality is suggested by ending in a plagal cadence or authentic cadence and also by simply ending on "I".

What are two characteristics of the harmonic phrase?
The harmonic phrase is usually 2-4 measures in length and is tied to the rhythmic and melodic phrase.

Lesson 4 Quiz

Log in to your course at www.udemy.com and take the quiz for this lesson.

Listening Assignments

Claude Debussy (1862 - 1918)

- Clair de Lune (Moonlight)
- Prélude à l'après-midi d'un faune (Prelude to the Afternoon of a Faun)
- Arabesque No. 1. Andantino con moto
- La fille aux cheveux de lin (The Girl with the Flaxen Hair)

Composition Assignments

Assignment 1

Compose a four measure harmonic phrase that suggests continuation and notate it using NotePad (or other notation software). You must end with a half cadence, dominant or dominant substitute. For a greater challenge, compose a melodic phrase to go with it. (Refer to *Music Composition 1* for melodic phrase writing.)

Assignment 2

Compose a four measure harmonic phrase that suggests continuation and notate it using NotePad (or other notation software). You must end with a pre-dominant or pre-dominant substitute. For a greater challenge, compose a melodic phrase to go with it. (Refer to *Music Composition 1* for melodic phrase writing.)

Assignment 3

Compose a four measure harmonic phrase that suggests temporary repose and notate it using NotePad (or other notation software). You must end with a deceptive cadence of "V" to "vi" or with one of the tonic substitutes. For a greater challenge, compose a melodic phrase to go with it. (Refer to *Music Composition 1* for melodic phrase writing.)

Assignment 4

Compose a four measure harmonic phrase that suggests finality and notate it using NotePad (or other notation software). You must end with a plagal cadence. For a greater challenge, compose a melodic phrase to go with it. (Refer to *Music Composition 1* for melodic phrase writing.)

Assignment 5

Compose a four measure harmonic phrase that suggests finality and notate it using NotePad (or other notation software). You must end with an authentic cadence. For a greater challenge, compose a melodic phrase to go with it. (Refer to *Music Composition 1* for melodic phrase writing.)

5. THE HARMONIC PERIOD

THE PERIOD

In the last lesson we learned about the different types of harmonic phrases. By combining phrases we can create **harmonic periods**. A harmonic period is two phrases that have an antecedent to consequent relationship. We call these phrases "question and answer" phrases.

The antecedent phrase (question phrase) is the weaker phrase and precedes the consequent phrase (answer phrase) which is strong. The strength of the phrase is determined by the cadence that ends the phrase.

The following diagram illustrates a typical harmonic period. As you can see, phrase 1 ends in a half cadence (HC) and is therefore an antecedent (question) phrase. Phrase 2 ends in a perfect authentic cadence (PAC) and is therefore a consequent (answer) phrase.

THE HARMONIC PERIOD

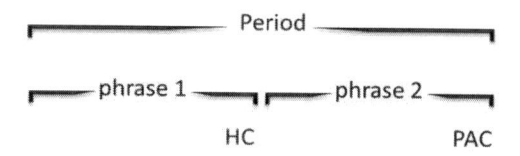

An antecedent to consequent relationship is said to exist as long as the second phrase is the stronger phrase. This is why some music theorists allow for phrase 1 to end with an imperfect authentic cadence (IAC), as long as phrase 2 ends with a perfect authentic cadence (PAC) which is the stronger of the two.

This excerpt from "Wild Rider" by Robert Schumann is an example of a period that follows the structure in the preceding diagram. Each phrase is four measures in length. The first line (phrase 1) ends with a half cadence (HC). This is a weak cadence and suggests a sense of continuation (a question). The second line (phrase 2) ends with a perfect authentic cadence (PAC). This is a strong cadence and suggests finality (the answer).

(Lesson 05 - Audio 01)

Note: When the melodic material is nearly the same in each phrase and changes only occur near the end of the second phrase, we call the answer phrase a "parallel answer" and the whole period a "parallel period". When the melodic material is different in each phrase we call the answer phrase a "contrasting answer" and the whole period a "contrasting period". The preceding excerpt from "Wild Rider" was an example of a parallel period since the melodic material in each phrase was nearly identical except for the final two notes.

THE PHRASE GROUP

When three phrases are combined we call it a **phrase group**. It is also sometimes referred to as a "three-phrase period". A phrase group does not technically have an antecedent to consequent relationship because there are either two questions and one answer, or one question and two answers. (The former is more common.) Once again, whether the phrase is a question or answer phrase is determined by the cadence.

The following diagram illustrates a typical phrase group. As you can see, both phrase 1 and phrase 2 end in half cadences and are therefore antecedent (question) phrases. Phrase 3 ends in a perfect authentic cadence and is therefore a consequent (answer) phrase.

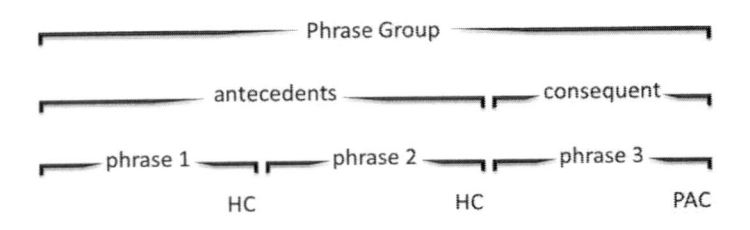

```
┌─────────────── Phrase Group ───────────────┐
┌─────────── antecedents ───────────┐ ┌─ consequent ─┐
┌── phrase 1 ──┐ ┌── phrase 2 ──┐ ┌── phrase 3 ──┐
       HC              HC              PAC
```

THE HARMONIC PERIOD

This arranged excerpt from "Voi, Che Sapete" from the *Marriage of Figaro* by Mozart is an example of a phrase group that follows the structure in the previous diagram. Each phrase is four measures in length. The cadences are marked beneath each line.

(Lesson 05 - Audio 02)

THE DOUBLE PERIOD

A **double period** contains four phrases. The first two phrases together form the antecedent (question) while the third and fourth phrases form the consequent (answer).

The following diagram illustrates a typical double period. What matters most are the cadences at the end of phrases 2 and 4.

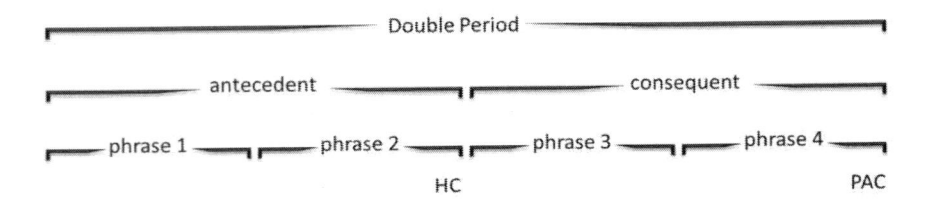

```
|─────────────────── Double Period ───────────────────|
|────── antecedent ──────|  |────── consequent ──────|
|─ phrase 1 ─| |─ phrase 2 ─| |─ phrase 3 ─| |─ phrase 4 ─|
                    HC                              PAC
```

Note: In a double period the cadence at the end of phrase 4 is almost always a PAC; the cadence at the end of phrase 2 is never a PAC; the cadences at the end of phrases 1 and 3 are also usually weak.

This excerpt from "Piano Sonata No. 12 in A flat major, Op. 26" by Beethoven is an example of a double period that follows the structure in the previous diagram. Each phrase is four measures in length. The cadences are marked beneath each line.

THE HARMONIC PERIOD

(Lesson 05 - Audio 03)

Note: This example is called a "parallel double period" because the melodic material in phrases 1 and 3 is nearly identical to the melodic material in phrases 2 and 4. This is very common in double periods.

Memory Questions

What is a harmonic period?
A harmonic period is two phrases that have an antecedent to consequent relationship.

The antecedent phrase is also called what?
The antecedent phrase is also called the question phrase.

The consequent phrase is also called what?
The consequent phrase is also called the answer phrase.

Is the antecedent the weaker or the stronger phrase?
The antecedent phrase is the weaker phrase and precedes the consequent phrase which is strong.

When does an antecedent to consequent relationship exist?
An antecedent to consequent relationship is said to exist as long as the second phrase is the stronger phrase.

How is the strength of the phrase determined?
The strength of the phrase is determined by the cadence that ends the phrase.

What is a phrase group?
A phrase group is a three-phrase period; there are either two antecedents and one consequent or one antecedent and two consequents.

What is a double period?
A double period contains four phrases; the first and second phrases form the antecedent while the third and fourth phrases form the consequent.

Lesson 5 Quiz

Log in to your course at www.udemy.com and take the quiz for this lesson.

Listening Assignments

Paul Dukas (1865 - 1935)

- The Sorcerer's Apprentice

Jean Sibelius (1865 - 1957)

- Finlandia

Erik Satie (1866 - 1925)

- Gymnopédie No. 1

Composition Assignments

Assignment 1

Compose a harmonic period consisting of two four-measure phrases and notate it using NotePad (or other notation software). The first phrase (antecedent) must end with a weak cadence. The second phrase (consequent) must end with a strong cadence. For a greater challenge, compose a melodic period to go with it. (Refer to *Music Composition 1* for melodic period writing.)

Assignment 2

Compose a phrase group (three-phrase period) and notate it using NotePad (or other notation software). It must consist of either two antecedents and one consequent or one antecedent and two consequents. For a greater challenge, compose a melody to go with it.

Assignment 3

Compose a double period consisting of four four-measure phrases and notate it using NotePad (or other notation software). The first and second phrases will be the antecedent phrases, while the third and fourth phrases will be the consequent phrases. For a greater challenge, compose a melody to go with it.

6. CHROMATIC CHORD SUBSTITUTION

BORROWED CHORDS

In lesson 2 we learned about diatonic chord substitution. We saw how certain chords within the key (diatonic chords) could be substituted for one another and take on each other's function as long as they had two pitches in common.

In this lesson we are going to learn how chords outside the key (chromatic chords) can be used as substitute chords. A very common form of chromatic chord substitution is substitution using **borrowed chords**. Borrowed chords are chords taken from the parallel key. Parallel keys are keys that share the same root. For example, "F major" and "F minor" are parallel keys because they share the same root "F".

Here is a diagram showing all of the chords from the parallel keys of "C major" which has no sharps or flats (first line) and "C minor" which has three flats: $B^\flat$, $E^\flat$, and $A^\flat$ (second line).

MUSIC COMPOSITION 2

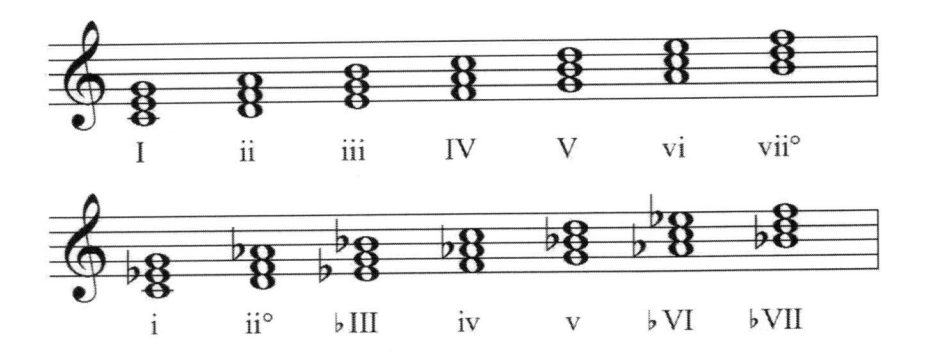

Chords that are directly above or below each other in the diagram can be easily substituted for one another (or "borrowed") since they share the same roots and/or because they have one to two notes in common.

Note: the Roman numerals under the chords in the second line are how the chords are named when they are used in the key of "C major" not how they are named in the key of "C minor". For example, the "III" chord is called a "flat III" because its root has been flatted. In the key of "C minor" this chord would simply be called "III".

Borrowed chords that share the same Roman numeral name are able to share the same function. For example, a "iv" chord from "C minor" could substitute for a "IV" chord in "C major" and it would continue to function as a "IV" (pre-dominant function). Listen to the following chord progression played first without the borrowed chord and then with the borrowed chord.

CHROMATIC CHORD SUBSTITUTION

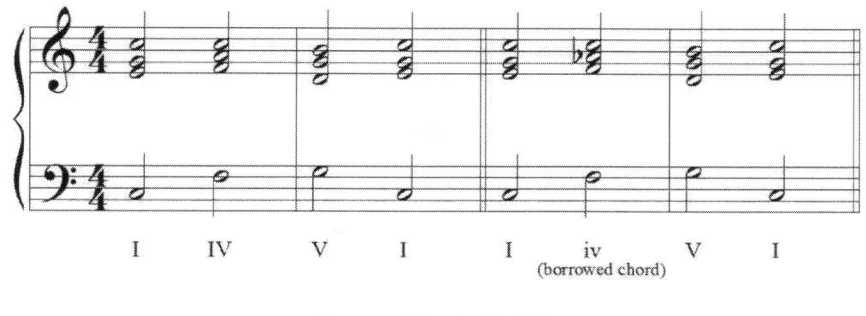

I   IV   V   I   I   iv   V   I
         (borrowed chord)

(Lesson 06 - Audio 01)

It is more common for a song in a major key to borrow chords from a minor key than a song in a minor key to borrow chords from a major key. This is because we have other forms of minor, such as the melodic minor scale (see *Music Theory* by the author), from which we can use pitches to create our chords. For example, with the pitches of the "C melodic minor" scale (C, D, E♭, F, G, A, and B) we can form all of the chords found in the "C major" scale with the exception of the tonic chord (C-E-G).

Here is an example of a chord progression in "C minor" that borrows the "I" chord from the parallel major "C major".

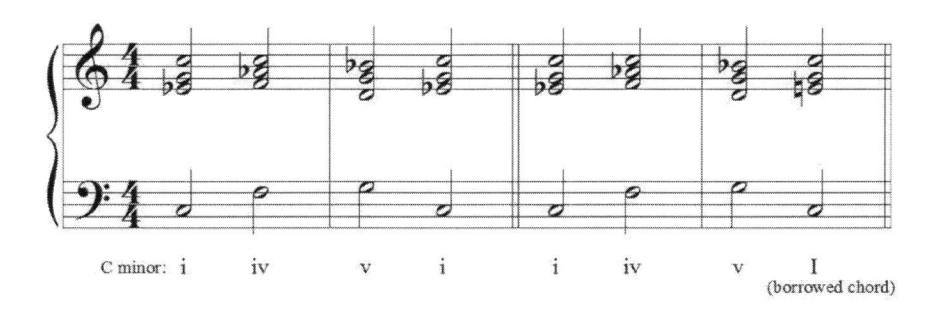

C minor: i   iv   v   i   i   iv   v   I
                                      (borrowed chord)

(Lesson 06 - Audio 02)

Note: When the expected minor tonic chord is changed to a major tonic chord it is referred to as a "Picardy third".

ALTERED CHORDS

Another type of chromatic chord substitution is substitution using **altered chords**. An altered chord is a chord that has one or more of its pitches replaced with a chromatic pitch not normally found in the key. Although at first glance this might seem to be the same thing as a borrowed chord, an altered chord differs from a borrowed chord in that it does not belong to the parallel key. The most common type of altered chord is the **secondary dominant**.

To understand secondary dominants we will need to study the following diagram. The first line consists of chords from the "C major" scale. The chords in the second line are all a perfect 5th higher than the chords directly above them (from the first line). The chords in the third line are the dominant seventh version of the chords directly above them (from the second line).

Secondary Dominants

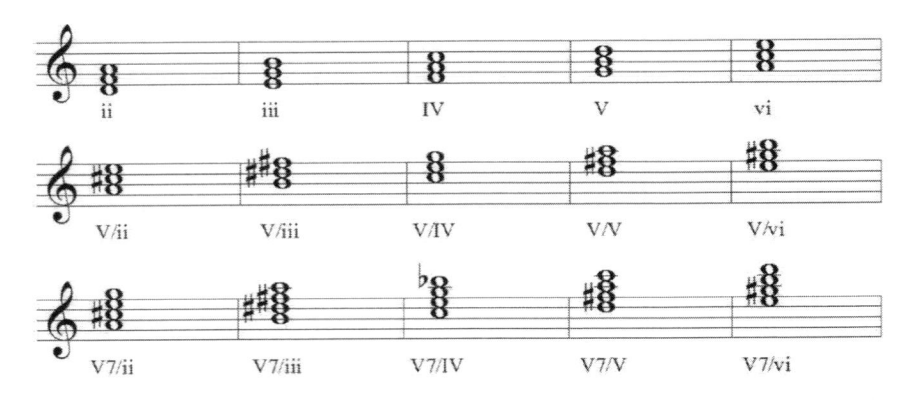

CHROMATIC CHORD SUBSTITUTION

Find the "V" chord in the first line and the chord directly below it in the second line called the "V/V". (We read this as "V of V") This "D major" chord is not normally found in the key of "C major", since there are no flats or sharps in the key of "C major". By altering the "F" to an "F sharp" we have created an "altered" chord.

When any chord in the second line is followed by the chord directly above it in the first line, the chord in the second line acts as a dominant function and the chord in the first line acts as a tonic function, that is, it is "tonicized". Tonicization is taking a chord that is not the tonic chord and making it temporarily sound as if it were a brand new tonic chord. This will be explained shortly when we look at a musical example which illustrates this.

The term "V of V" can be confusing so let's explain further before we look at a chord progression which uses a "V of V". Here is a diagram that will help to illustrate. The first line is how we would name the chords in the key of "C major", and the second line is how we would name the same chords in the key of "G major".

C	G	D
I	V	V/V
	I	V

As you can see, the "G major" chord is the "V" chord in relation to the key of "C major" (first line), but a "I" chord in relation to the key of "G major" (second line). The "D major" chord is the "V" chord in relation to the key of "G major" (second line) but a "V of V" in relation to the key of "C major" (first line). When composers use secondary dominant chords in their compositions, they are taking a chord from another key and bringing it into the current key where it does not normally belong.

V/V is also referred to as the "dominant of the dominant". In other words, "G" is the dominant of "C", and "D" is the dominant of "G", therefore, "D" is the dominant of the dominant as it relates to "C".

Let's look at a musical example. Here is a chord progression that uses the altered chord "V/V".

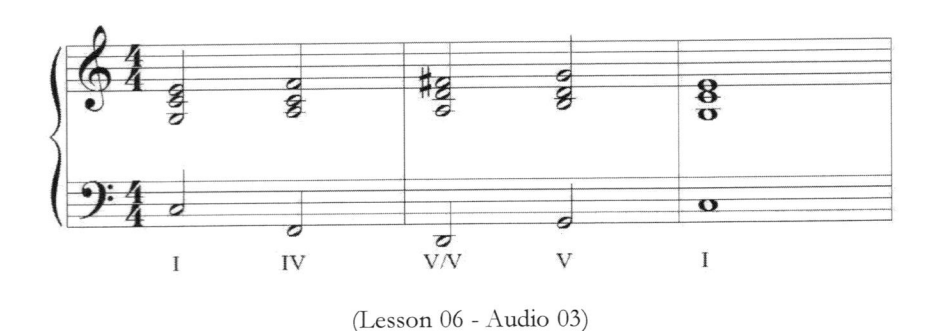

(Lesson 06 - Audio 03)

Since there are no "F sharps" in the key of "C major", the third chord in this progression would have normally been a "D minor" chord (ii) and would have acted as a pre-dominant substitute. Because of the altered pitch (the "F sharp") it is now a "D major" chord and acts as a dominant of the dominant, thus tonicizing the "G major" chord which follows it. For only a brief moment we feel as if the "G major" chord is actually the "I" chord. Because the chord that follows is a "C major" chord (the "true" tonic), this feeling is short lived. Do you see how the "V" chord has a dual function here? It acts as a tonic (I) in relation to the chord that preceded it, but as a dominant (V) in relation to the chord that follows it.

Here is another example of a chord progression that uses a secondary dominant. This time we have chosen to use the "V of ii". If you look back at the diagram of secondary dominants from this lesson you will see that the "ii" chord in the key of "C major" is the "D minor" chord. This chord's dominant (a perfect 5th above it) is the "A

CHROMATIC CHORD SUBSTITUTION

major" chord (directly below it on the diagram).

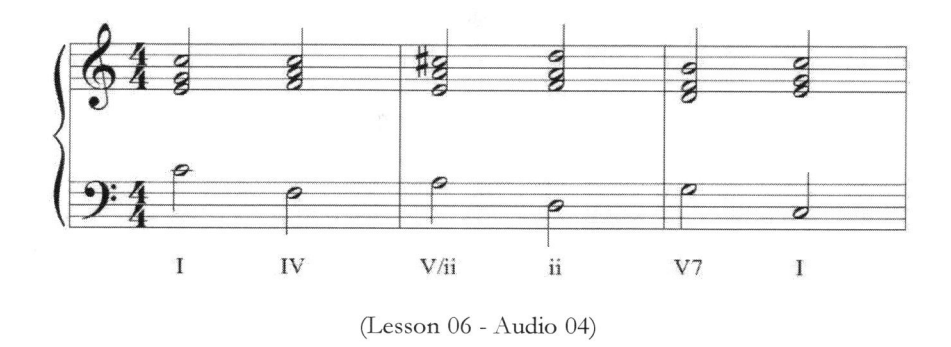

I   IV   V/ii   ii   V7   I

(Lesson 06 - Audio 04)

Since there are no "C sharps" in the key of "C major", the third chord in this progression would have normally been an "A minor" chord (vi) and would have acted as a tonic substitute. Because of the altered pitch (the "C sharp") it is now an "A major" chord and acts as a dominant of the "ii" chord, thus tonicizing the "D minor" chord which follows it. For only a brief moment we feel as if the "D minor" chord is actually the "i" chord. Because the chord that follows is a "G7" chord, this feeling is short lived.

Here are some tips to follow when using secondary dominants in your chord progressions.

1. A secondary dominant will typically be preceded by a chord that has one or two notes in common with it. (see both preceding musical examples)
2. A secondary dominant chord will always be followed by the chord of which it is the dominant. (A "V of iii" will be followed by a "iii"; a "V of vi" will be followed by a "vi", etc.)

Note: In the diagram of secondary dominants at the beginning of this section, you may have noticed that the "V/IV" is completely identical to the tonic chord of the key (C major). Due to this fact the "V of

IV" is never used as a secondary dominant. Instead the "V⁷/IV" is used in its place in order to make clear the secondary dominant function. Also take note that there was no "V/vii°" chord in the diagram. Secondary dominants "tonicize" the chord of which they are the dominant. The "vii°" chord is a diminished chord and is therefore not able to be "tonicized" (tonic chords can only be major or minor).

Here is a diagram of all of the secondary dominants in a minor key. The first line consists of chords from the "A minor" scale. The chords in the second line are all a perfect 5th higher than the chords directly above them (from the first line). The chords in the third line are the dominant seventh version of the chords directly above them (from the second line).

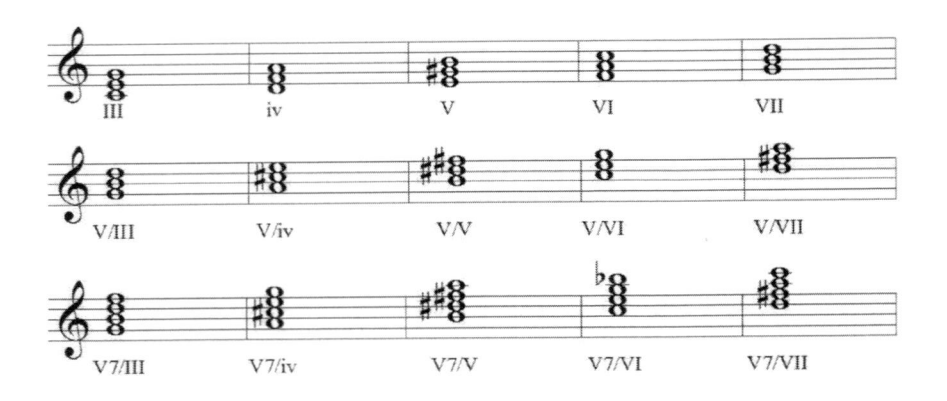

III	iv	V	VI	VII
V/III	V/iv	V/V	V/VI	V/VII
V7/III	V7/iv	V7/V	V7/VI	V7/VII

Note: The "V/VI" is completely identical to the "III" and is therefore not used as a secondary dominant. Instead the "V⁷/VI" is used in its place in order to make clear the secondary dominant function. Although the "V/III" is completely identical to the "VII" chord, it is often used as a secondary dominant function when moving to the relative major key of "C major". Also take note that there was no "V/ii°" chord in the diagram. Again, secondary dominants "tonicize" the chord of which they are the dominant. The "ii°" chord is a diminished chord and is therefore not able to be "tonicized" (tonic chords can only be major or minor).

Memory Questions

What is a diatonic chord?
A diatonic chord is a chord made up of pitches within the key.

What is a chromatic chord?
A chromatic chord is a chord that includes one or more pitches from outside the key.

What are borrowed chords?
Borrowed chords are chords taken from the parallel key.

What is a parallel key?
A parallel key is one that shares the same root with another key.

What function do borrowed chords have?
Borrowed chords that share the same Roman numeral name are able to share the same function.

What is an altered chord?
An altered chord is a chord that has one or more of its pitches replaced with a chromatic pitch not normally found in the key.

How does an altered chord differ from a borrowed chord?
An altered chord differs from a borrowed chord in that it does not belong to the parallel key.

What is the most common type of altered chord?
The most common type of altered chord is the secondary dominant.

What is a secondary dominant?
A secondary dominant is the dominant of the dominant.

What function do secondary dominants have?
Secondary dominants tonicize the chord of which they are the dominant.

What is tonicization?
Tonicization is taking a chord that is not the tonic chord and making it temporarily sound as if it were a brand new tonic chord.

Lesson 6 Quiz

Log in to your course at www.udemy.com and take the quiz for this lesson.

Listening Assignments

Franz Lehár (1870 - 1948)
- Overture to the operetta "The Merry Widow"

Sergei Rachmaninoff (1873 - 1943)

- Prelude in D major, Op. 23, No. 4
- Piano Concerto No. 2 in C minor, Op. 18

Composition Assignments

Assignment 1

Log into your course at www.udemy.com. You will find the assignments for this lesson in section 6 under the "Downloadable Materials" tab. Print the .pdf file "**Lesson 06_Assignment 01**". The first line is the original progression. The second line is the same progression with a borrowed chord used in place of one of the chords. Instructions: Fill in the missing borrowed chord from the parallel minor key. The Roman numeral is provided for you. You must also fill in the missing bass note with the root of the borrowed chord. When you are finished, compare your progression with the progression in the answer key "**Lesson 06_Assignment 01 Answer Key**" which can also be found under the "Downloadable Materials" tab.

Assignment 2

Log into your course at www.udemy.com. You will find the assignments for this lesson in section 6 under the "Downloadable Materials" tab. Print the .pdf file "**Lesson 06_Assignment 02**". The first line is the original progression. The second line is the same progression with a borrowed chord used in place of one of the chords. Instructions: Fill in the missing borrowed chord from the parallel minor key. The Roman numeral is provided for you. You must also fill in the missing bass note with the root of the borrowed chord. When you are finished, compare your progression with the progression in the answer key "**Lesson 06_Assignment 02 Answer Key**" which can also be found under the "Downloadable Materials" tab.

Assignment 3

Log into your course at www.udemy.com. You will find the assignments for this lesson in section 6 under the "Downloadable Materials" tab. Print the .pdf file "**Lesson 06_Assignment 03**". The first line is the original progression. The second line is the same progression with multiple borrowed chords used in place of some of the chords. Instructions: Fill in the missing borrowed chords from the parallel minor key. The Roman numerals are provided for you. You must also fill in the missing bass notes with the roots of the borrowed chords. When you are finished, compare your progression with the progression in the answer key "**Lesson 06_Assignment 03 Answer Key**" which can also be found under the "Downloadable Materials" tab.

Assignment 4

Log into your course at www.udemy.com. You will find the assignments for this lesson in section 6 under the "Downloadable Materials" tab. Print the .pdf file "**Lesson 06_Assignment 04**". The first line is the original progression. The second line is the same progression with multiple borrowed chords used in place of some of the chords. Instructions: Fill in the missing borrowed chords from the parallel minor key. The Roman numerals are provided for you. You must also fill in the missing bass notes with the roots of the borrowed chords. When you are finished, compare your progression

CHROMATIC CHORD SUBSTITUTION

with the progression in the answer key "**Lesson 06_Assignment 04 Answer Key**" which can also be found under the "Downloadable Materials" tab.

Assignment 5

Notate the following chord progression in the key of "G major" using NotePad (or other notation software): I - V7/IV - IV - V - I. You may include a bass line if you wish.

Assignment 6

Notate the following chord progression in the key of "F major" using NotePad (or other notation software): I - V7/IV - IV - V - vi - V/V - V - I. You may include a bass line if you wish.

Assignment 7

Compose a chord progression in the key of "C major" that includes the secondary dominant "V/vi" and notate it using NotePad (or other notation software). You may include a bass line if you wish.

7. MODULATION

PIVOT CHORDS

Modulation is changing from one key to a different key within a single movement of a piece. (Key change between movements in a larger piece with multiple movements is not modulation but rather "change of key".) When music modulates to a new key, a new key signature may or may not be used. This is up to the composer and is usually determined by how long the piece will stay in the new key. If the piece stays in the new key for only a short while, accidentals will typically be used in the music rather than changing the key signature.

Modulation satisfies the compositional principle of "variety" and brings the change necessary to keep a piece from becoming repetitive and boring. Modulation can also help to delineate the different sections of a piece. (We will talk about this further when we study compositional form.)

Modulation is a complicated compositional technique and a vast topic. Since this is a beginning composition course, we will be looking primarily at modulation to related keys. Related keys are keys that are closer to each other on the Circle of 5ths, such as the dominant key (V), the subdominant key (IV), as well as the relative major or relative minor keys. We will now proceed to look at some of the more common ways of modulating.

There are many ways to modulate, but all of them involve the establishment of a new tonic chord (a new "I" chord). When a new chord is used as the tonic chord for a very short period of time (usually less than a phrase) it is considered "tonicization" rather than modulation. We saw examples of this in lesson 6 when we discussed secondary dominants.

One of the most common ways to modulate is through use of **pivot chords** (also known as "common-chords"). Pivot chords are chords that are common to two different keys (the key you are starting in and the key you are modulating to). To find the chords that two keys share in common simply line up all of the chords of the two keys. Here is a diagram showing the chords that are common to both the key of "C major" and the key of "B flat major".

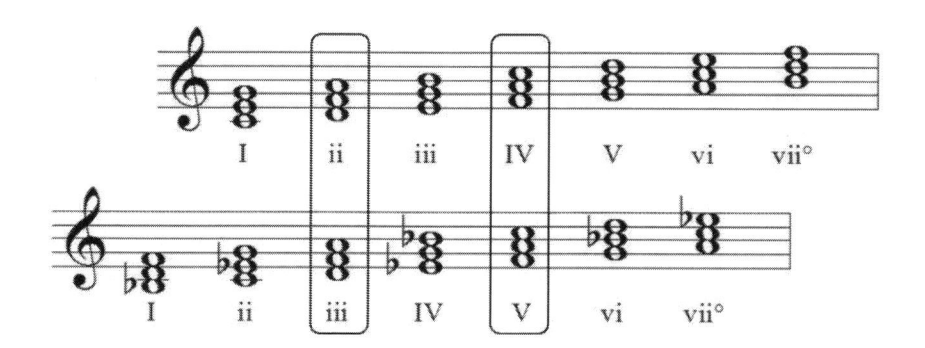

As you can see in the preceding diagram, the "D minor" chord and "F major" chord are the only chords that are common to both the key of "C major" and the key of "B flat major". These chords are therefore called "common-chords" and can be used to pivot between the key of "C major" and the key of "B flat major". We will look at a musical example that uses the common-chord "D minor" momentarily.

When using pivot chords to modulate from one key to another it is important to remember that keys further apart on the Circle of 5ths have fewer chords in common. Take for example the following keys from the Circle of 5ths.

$$B^\flat - F - \mathbf{C} - G - D$$

The key of "C major" will have four chords in common with the key a 5th to the right (G major), but only 2 chords in common with the key two 5ths to the right (D major). The same thing happens when we go left on the Circle of 5ths. The key of "C major" will have four chords in common with the key a 5th to the left (F major), but only 2 chords in common with the key two 5ths to the left (B♭ major). Once you go beyond two 5ths on the circle in either direction there are no shared chords with "C major".

There are three steps to modulation using pivot chords.

1. A tonic must already be firmly established.
2. A pivot chord is used and the tonal center begins to change.
3. A new tonic is firmly established and made clear to the listener.

Listen to the following musical example.

MODULATION

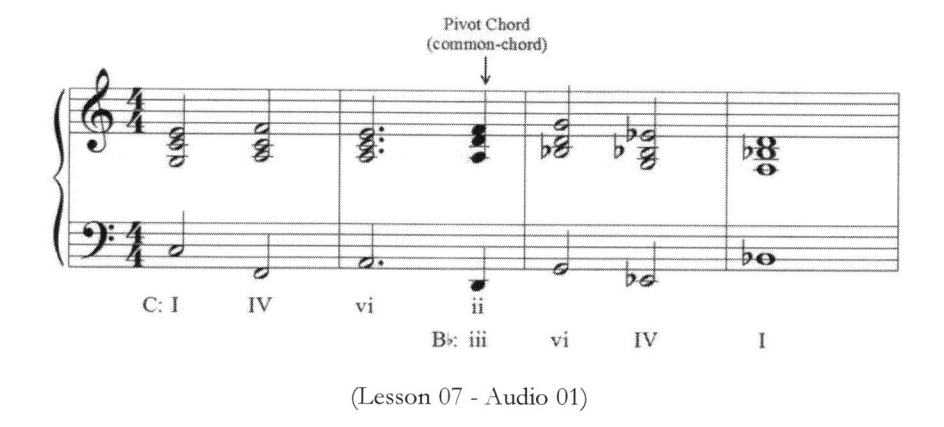

(Lesson 07 - Audio 01)

Let's analyze this excerpt and see where each of the three steps of modulation through use of a pivot chord was followed. We will assume that the tonic "C" has already been firmly established by any preceding musical material. A pivot chord (the D minor chord) is used in the second measure. This is the point at which the tonal center begins to change. The new tonal center is not yet clear to the listener until a tonic chord is firmly established. Typically a new tonic is established by means of a cadence. In this example, a plagal cadence (IV to I) helps to firmly establish the "B flat" chord as the new tonic chord. It is at this point in the music that the listener knows we are in the new key of "B flat major".

MODULATION USING ALTERED CHORDS

We learned about altered chords in lesson 6. Altered chords are chords that have one or more of their pitches replaced with pitches not found in the key. We saw how a particular type of altered chord called a "secondary dominant", was able to make a chord that is not the tonic chord sound as if it were the tonic chord for a brief period of time before returning to the original tonic. When we do not return to the original tonic chord we have modulated to a new key.

Here is an example of an altered chord (that is also a secondary dominant) being used to modulate. This excerpt is taken from "Sonata No. 10 in G Major, Op. 14" by Beethoven.

G: V   I   ii   V7/V
                         D: V7   I

(Lesson 07 - Audio 02)

This example begins in the key of "G major" and modulates to the key of "D major". The altered chord can be found in the second half of measure four where the "ii" chord has been altered from "A minor" to "A major" by means of the "C sharp". The "G" in the right hand actually makes the chord into a dominant seventh chord ("A^7"). This "A^7" chord is a "V^7" in relation to the destination key of "D major" but a "V^7 of V" in relation to the starting key of "G major".

Although this altered chord acts as a pivot chord it cannot technically be called one since the "A^7" chord is not shared between the keys of "G major" and "D major". The "A^7" chord belongs solely to the key of "D major"; it is only loosely related to the key of "G major" by being a secondary dominant.

PIVOT TONE MODULATION

Another type of modulation similar to pivot chord modulation (common-chord modulation) is **pivot tone modulation** or "common-tone modulation". The differentiating factor is that pivot chord modulation uses a <u>chord</u> that is common to both the starting key and the destination key in order to modulate, whereas pivot tone modulation uses a <u>single tone</u> that is common to both the starting key and the destination key in order to modulate. Listen to the following excerpt from "Fantasy No. 4 in C minor, K. 475" by W. A. Mozart.

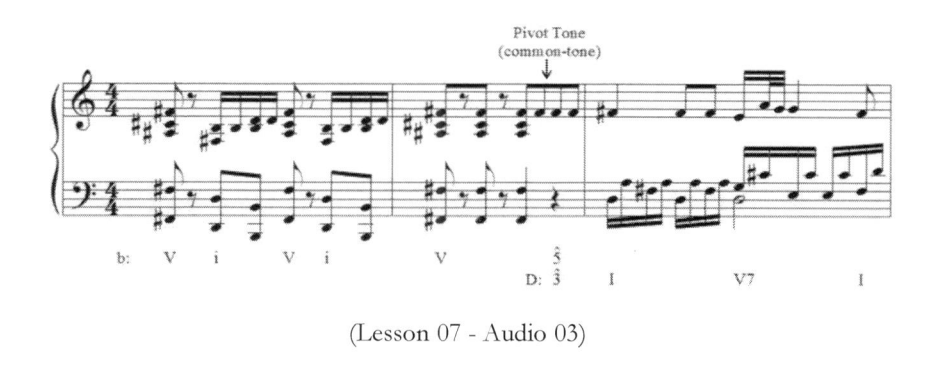

(Lesson 07 - Audio 03)

This example begins in the key of "B minor" and modulates to the key of "D major". The "F sharp" is a tone that is common to both keys. It is the fifth pitch of the "B minor" scale and the third pitch of the "D major" scale. When our ears hear the "F sharp" in isolation it's not that we forget the preceding tonality, but rather, our ears are open to the possibility of other tonalities that can grow out of that single tone.

SEQUENTIAL MODULATION

In lesson 11 of *Music Composition 1* we studied the different types of melodic sequences. Chromatic sequences (non-diatonic sequences) can actually be a great tool for modulating to other keys. Here is an example from the 1st movement of "Sonata No. 21 in C Major, Op. 53" by Beethoven.

(Lesson 07 - Audio 04)

This example begins in the key of "C major" and modulates to the key of "B flat major". The second line is an exact restatement of the first four measures, only a whole step lower in pitch. This type of modulation is very easily accomplished and is fairly common.

DIRECT MODULATION

Another type of modulation is **direct modulation**. It is sometimes called "abrupt modulation" because there is no "set up" for it. There is no use of pivot chords, pivot tones, altered chords or sequences to help smooth out the modulation; it happens abruptly. Because this type of modulation typically occurs between two phrases it is also referred to as "phrase modulation". Listen to the following example from the 2nd movement of "Sonata in C major" by Tobias Haslinger.

(Lesson 07 - Audio 05)

This example begins in the key of "C major" and modulates to the key of "G major". The first line ends decidedly in the key of "C major" with an authentic cadence (V^7 to I). The next phrase begins in the key of "G major" without any signs or warning. Direct modulation is not only used between phrases, it is also often commonly used between sections of a song. The preceding musical excerpt is an example of this. We shall learn about sections of a song in lesson 10 when we begin the study of compositional form.

Memory Questions

What is modulation?
Modulation is changing from one key to a different key within a single movement of a piece.

What do all types of modulation involve?
All types of modulation involve the establishment of a new tonic chord.

What is a pivot chord?
A pivot chord is a chord that is common to both the key you are starting in and the key you are modulating to.

What is a pivot tone?
A pivot tone is a tone that is common to both the key you are starting in and the key you are modulating to.

What is sequential modulation?
Sequential modulation is modulation through a chromatic sequence.

What is direct modulation?
Direct modulation is modulation that is abrupt; it does not use pivot chords, pivot tones, altered chords or sequences to help smooth out the modulation.

Why is direct modulation also referred to as "phrase modulation"?
Direct modulation is also referred to as phrase modulation because this type of modulation typically occurs between two phrases.

Lesson 7 Quiz

Log in to your course at www.udemy.com and take the quiz for this lesson.

Listening Assignments

Ottorino Respighi (1879 - 1936)

- Pines of Rome

Ralph Vaughan Williams (1872 - 1958)

- Symphony No. 2 "A London Symphony"

Composition Assignments

Assignment 1

Modulate from the key of "C major" to the key of "D major" using a pivot chord. Include a bass line, or for a greater challenge compose a melody to go with the chord progression. Notate using NotePad (or other notation software).

Assignment 2

Modulate from the key of "G major" to the key of "B flat major" using a pivot tone. Be sure to include a melody as this is where the pivot tone will be used. Notate using NotePad (or other notation software).

Assignment 3

Modulate from the key of "C major" to the key of "A major" using an altered chord. Do not use an altered chord that is a secondary dominant. Do not use a borrowed chord. Include a bass line, or for a greater challenge compose a melody to go with the chord progression. Notate using NotePad (or other notation software).

Assignment 4

Modulate from the key of "F major" to the key of "D major" using sequence modulation. Be sure to include a melodic sequence with the chord progression that you sequence. Notate the sequence using NotePad (or other notation software).

Assignment 5

Modulate from the key of "A major" to the key of "D major" using direct ("phrase") modulation. Compose two phrases. Each phrase should consist of a melody and a chord progression. End the first phrase in the key of "A major" and begin the second phrase in the key of "D major". Notate using NotePad (or other notation software).

8. HARMONIC RHYTHM

FREQUENCEY OF CHORD CHANGES

In this lesson we are going to take a look at **harmonic rhythm**. The term harmonic rhythm can be a little misleading. It is not the rhythm to which the chords are played. For example, the "F major" chord in the following diagram has a definite rhythm, but this is not the "harmonic" rhythm.

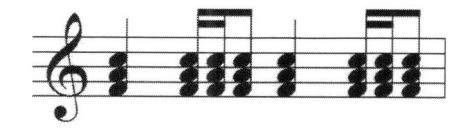

Harmonic rhythm is "the rate at which the chord changes take place". Since there are no chord changes in the preceding example this is not harmonic rhythm. It is simply the rhythm of the chords. Here is an example to help illustrate harmonic rhythm.

MUSIC COMPOSITION 2

(Lesson 08 - Audio 01)

The chord progression in the preceding diagram is "i - V - i". The rate at which the chords change is: one measure of "D minor", two measures of "A major", and one measure of "D minor". This is the harmonic rhythm.

Now that you have studied a little bit about chord progressions, the next question to ask is "how often should I change chords?" Should I change chords once every measure? Should I change chords once every beat? Should I keep the same harmonic rhythm for the entire piece? There are no right or wrong answers to these questions. The frequency of the chord changes depends on what is happening in the melody and the pacing and mood the composer is trying to create.

Let's take a look at a simple example using "Mary Had A Little Lamb".

HARMONIC RHYTHM

(Lesson 08 - Audio 02)

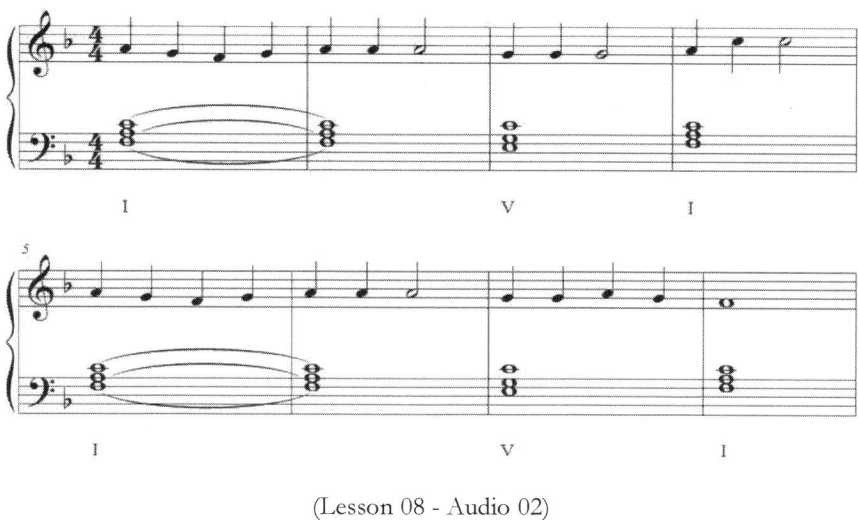

As you can see, the harmonic rhythm is slow and not very interesting. Let's take the same song and increase the rate at which the chords change and see what happens. (We'll also throw in some substitute chords to spice this familiar tune up a bit!)

(Lesson 08 - Audio 03)

MUSIC COMPOSITION 2

As you can hear, the harmonic rhythm is now faster and the song is a bit more interesting.

Here are a few rules of thumb for deciding on the harmonic rhythm. Remember, these are simply guidelines to help you in the composing process and are not meant as rules that cannot be broken.

1. Avoid changing chords for every single note in the melody. When the chords change with every note in the melody, the melodic rhythm and the harmonic rhythm will match exactly. When this happens there is no contrast between the melodic line and the harmonic line. This becomes very tedious sounding and typically you should try and avoid this (unless it is intentional and you want your piece to be more "chordal" in nature). Here is an example in which the melodic rhythm and harmonic rhythm coincide. (The melody is the top voice in the treble clef.)

(Lesson 08 - Audio 04)

2. Have chord changes occur on stronger beats. Since most music is metered, it is very common to find that chord changes occur on the stronger beats, such as the first beat of the measure and/or the mid-beat of the measure (beats one and three in 4/4 meter; beats one and four in 6/8 meter). Here is an example of the chords changing on the strong beats in 4/4 meter.

HARMONIC RHYTHM

(Lesson 08 - Audio 05)

3. Give slower paced melodies a faster paced harmonic rhythm (and vice versa). When the melodic line is made up of notes of longer duration (such as whole notes and half notes) the harmonic rhythm is the driving force and the melody takes a back seat. In the following example, all the rhythmic activity is in the harmony via the six chord changes. Notice how three of the chord changes occur during the duration of the first note in the treble clef. (The first note in the treble clef is a chord tone in each of the first three chords allowing each of the three chords to harmonize with it.)

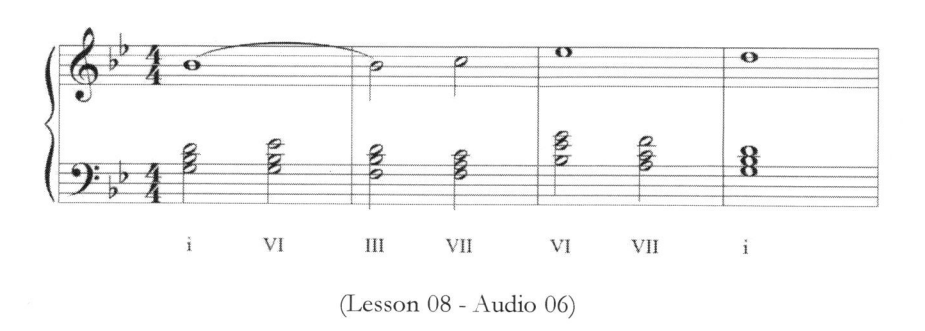

(Lesson 08 - Audio 06)

When the melodic line is made up of notes of shorter duration (such as 8th notes and 16th notes) the melody is the driving force and the harmonic rhythm takes a back seat. In the following example, all the rhythmic activity is in the melody; there is only one chord change.

(Lesson 08 - Audio 07)

4. Vary the harmonic rhythm. Don't use the same harmonic rhythm for an entire phrase, period, or section of a piece. (We will learn about "sections" in lesson 10 when we begin the study of compositional form.) For example, if the chords are changing at a rate of once per measure for the first four measures, don't keep doing this in perpetuity…use the principle of variety to keep things interesting!

Memory Questions

What is harmonic rhythm?
Harmonic rhythm is the rate at which the chord changes take place.

How frequently should chord changes take place?
The frequency of the chord changes depends on what is happening in the melody and the pacing and mood the composer is trying to create.

Lesson 8 Quiz

Log in to your course at www.udemy.com and take the quiz for this lesson.

Listening Assignments

Gustav Holst (1874 - 1934)

- The Planets

Composition Assignments

Assignment 1

Log into your course at www.udemy.com. You will find the assignments for this lesson in section 8 under the "Downloadable Materials" tab. Print the .pdf file "**Lesson 08_Assignment 01**". In this assignment you will be writing three different harmonic rhythms for the same melody. Instructions: Harmonize the melody in line 1 using only one chord change per measure. Harmonize the same melody in line 2 using two chords changes per measure. Harmonize the same melody in line 3 using a chord change for every note in the melody.

Assignment 2

Compose a slower paced melody with a faster paced harmonic rhythm 1-2 phrases in length. Notate using NotePad (or other notation software).

Assignment 3

Compose a faster paced melody with a slower paced harmonic rhythm 1-2 phrases in length. Notate using NotePad (or other notation software).

9. MUSICAL TEXTURE

HOMOPHONIC TEXTURE

In this lesson we are going to look at musical texture. Musical texture is the way in which rhythm, melody and harmony are combined. We have already touched upon how melody is tied to harmony when we studied chord tones and non-chord tones in *Music Composition 1*. (It would be very beneficial at this point to review lessons 17-20 in *Music Composition 1* before completing the assignments for this lesson.)

The first musical texture we are going to look at is called **homophonic**. Homophonic comes from the Greek word "homophōnos" meaning "same sounds". Music with a homophonic texture is music that has a single melodic line with a harmonic accompaniment.

Let's look at some examples of common harmonic accompaniments found in music. As you study these examples, remember that the melody can be made up of just chord tones, or a combination of chord tones and non-chord tones (*Music Composition 1*, lessons 17-20).

BLOCK CHORD ACCOMPANIMENT

Block chord accompaniment is the most basic type of accompaniment. A block chord is a chord in which the pitches are played simultaneously. There are two block chords in the following example.

(Lesson 09 - Audio 01)

A block chord can be held until the next chord change as it was in the preceding example. A block chord can also be played repeatedly in various rhythmic patterns until the next chord change as in the following example. This is much more interesting and allows the harmony to contribute to the rhythmic element of a piece.

(Lesson 09 - Audio 02)

MUSICAL TEXTURE

It is not necessary that all three pitches of a chord be played in the accompaniment. Sometimes composers will use just two pitches from a chord, thus allowing the listener's ears to "infer" the third pitch. Other times the third pitch will occur somewhere in the melody as it does in the following example.

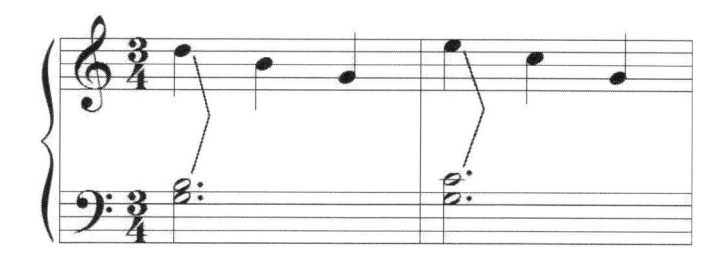

(Lesson 09 - Audio 03)

The chord heard in the first measure is a "G major" chord. The "D" in the melody is the missing pitch from the chord in the left hand and completes the chord. The chord heard in the second measure is a "C major" chord. The "E" in the melody is the missing pitch from the chord in the left hand and completes the chord.

Note: The pitch in the melody that completes the chord does not have to occur on the same beat with the chord; it can occur at any place in the melody while the chord is being heard.

Before moving on we will mention one other way that block chords can be used to accompany a melody. Rather than repeating the same chord over and over again, inversions of the chord are sometimes used. Here is an example of a possible left hand accompaniment using inversions of the "C major" chord.

BROKEN CHORD ACCOMPANIMENT

A broken chord is a chord in which the pitches are played sequentially. Broken chords are also sometimes referred to as "arpeggiated" chords (from the Italian "arpeggiare", meaning "to play on the harp"). There are many kinds of broken chord accompaniments. In this section of the lesson we will look at some of the more common types.

A very common type of broken chord accompaniment popular in the Classical period (and also into the Romantic period) was **Alberti Bass** (named after Domenico Alberti because he used it quite frequently). In Alberti Bass, the pitches of each chord are played in the pattern: "lowest - highest - middle - highest". For example, the "C major" chord in the first measure of the following excerpt is played: "C-G-E-G".

(Lesson 09 - Audio 04)

Typically Alberti Bass occurs in the left hand of piano music and uses notes of shorter duration than the notes in the melody. (Although it is typical in piano music for the melody to be in the right hand and the harmony in the left hand, this is not a necessity. Many examples exist where the melody is in the left hand and the harmony is in the right hand.)

Arranging the pitches of the chord in the pattern: "lowest - highest - middle - highest", such as in Alberti Bass, is not the only way pitches of a broken chord can be arranged. There are countless other ways that the pitches of a chord can be played sequentially. Here is a diagram showing some common examples. Let's look at each line in turn.

1. This example uses the arrangement: "lowest - middle - highest - middle".
2. This example uses an extended version of the chord with the root being played again an octave higher.
3. This example uses both an ascending and descending extended version of the chord.
4. This example uses the arrangement: "lowest - middle - highest".
5. This example uses "open harmony" where the highest and lowest pitches of the chord are more than an octave apart.
6. This example uses open harmony with multiple types of note durations.

Another type of broken chord accompaniment is the **waltz accompaniment**. In a waltz accompaniment the lowest note of the chord is played alone on the first beat, while the middle and highest notes are played together on the second and third beats. (A waltz is typically in 3/4 meter)

(Lesson 09 - Audio 05)

Note: Although two pitches of the chord are played simultaneously this is still considered a broken chord rather than a block chord since not all three pitches are played simultaneously.

Pieces in meters other than 3/4 may have accompaniments similar to a waltz accompaniment as in the following example.

(Lesson 09 - Audio 06)

As with any harmonic accompaniment we can always create variation through change in the rhythmic structure. Here is an example.

Another variation involves the inserting of another pitch of the chord as an alternate bass note on the third beat.

These are just a few of countless possibilities for broken chord accompaniments. You will be asked to experiment and come up with some of your own broken chord accompaniments for one of the lesson assignments.

HOMORHYTHMIC TEXTURE

A **homorhythmic** texture is similar to a homophonic texture except that the melody and the accompaniment have the same rhythm. This is common in choral music but can also be found in many piano pieces. Here is an example.

(Lesson 09 - Audio 07)

The melody can be found in the highest pitches of the right hand. The lower pitches in the right hand and the pitches in the left hand form the harmony. Because both the melody and the harmony share the same rhythm this musical excerpt is categorized as homorhythmic.

POLYPHONIC TEXTURE

The musical texture we are going to look at in this section is called **polyphonic**. Polyphonic comes from the Greek word "polyphōnia", meaning "many sounds". Music with a polyphonic texture is music that has multiple melodic lines able to stand on their own independent of each other, but when taken together form the harmony of the piece.

Although polyphonic writing is very complex and goes beyond the scope of a beginning course in music composition, let's take a quick look at one very simple example so that you are familiar with the basic concept.

MUSICAL TEXTURE

(Lesson 09 - Audio 08)

As you can see, the left hand is not playing chords but rather a bass line that is melodic in nature. Both the right hand and the left hand could be played separately and could stand on their own independent of each other, but when taken together they form harmonies between the two of them. For example, the pitches in the first half of measure 7 when taken together form the pitches of a "C major" chord. The pitches in the second half of measure 7 when taken together form the pitches of a "G Major" chord. Music has a horizontal aspect (melody) and a vertical aspect (harmony). Composers must think both horizontally and vertically when writing music.

OTHER ACCOMPANIMENTS

Two other accompaniments that are worth mentioning are **pedal point** and **ostinato**. A pedal point is a single pitch that is held for all or most of a piece. It is typically a tonic or dominant pitch played in the bass. When two pedal points occur together it is called a "double pedal point".

(Lesson 09 - Audio 09)

As you can see, the preceding example uses a double pedal point (the tonic and dominant pitch of "G major"). Since the pedal point does not change pitch, some of the notes in the melody will be consonant with the pedal point and some of the notes in the melody will be dissonant with the pedal point.

And finally let's look at the "ostinato". The word ostinato comes from the Italian word meaning "stubborn" or "obstinate". An ostinato is a motif or phrase that is repeated in a very persistent manner. When an ostinato occurs in a bass line it is called a "bass ostinato". Listen to the bass ostinato in the left hand of the following example.

(Lesson 09 - Audio 10)

This ostinato consists of the pitches "A", "E" a 5th above, "E" an 8th below, and "E" an 8th above again. Since this pattern was repeated very persistently in each measure, it is therefore considered an ostinato and not simply a motif that reoccurred a couple of times.

Memory Questions

What is musical texture?
Musical texture is the way in which rhythm, melody and harmony are combined.

What is a homophonic texture?
A homophonic texture is a single melodic line with a harmonic accompaniment.

All harmonic accompaniments fall into what two groups?
All harmonic accompaniments are either block accompaniments or broken accompaniments.

What is a homorhythmic texture?
A homorhythmic texture is melody and accompaniment that have the same rhythm.

What is a polyphonic texture?
A polyphonic texture is multiple melodic lines which together form the harmony of the piece.

What is a pedal point?
A pedal point is a single pitch that is held for all or most of a piece.

Pedal points are typically which pitch of the scale?
Pedal points are typically a tonic or dominant pitch.

What is a double pedal point?
A double pedal point is two pedal points that occur together.

What is an ostinato?
An ostinato is a motif or phrase that is repeated in a very persistent manner.

Lesson 9 Quiz

Log in to your course at www.udemy.com and take the quiz for this lesson.

Listening Assignments

Maurice Ravel (1875 - 1937)

- Pavane pour une infante défunte (Pavane for a Dead Princess) Listen to piano version & orchestral version.
- String Quartet in F major
- Daphnis et Chloé Suite No. 2

Composition Assignments

Assignment 1

Log into your course at www.udemy.com. You will find the assignments for this lesson in section 9 under the "Downloadable Materials" tab. Print the .pdf file "**Lesson 09_Assignment 01**". Instructions: Compose three different block chord accompaniments for the same melody. (Line one is the original melody and accompaniment.) Hint: use the exact same chords but alter the rhythm in which the chords are played. This will change the rhythmic texture and thus the overall texture of the music.

Assignment 2

Log into your course at www.udemy.com. You will find the assignments for this lesson in section 9 under the "Downloadable Materials" tab. Print the .pdf file "**Lesson 09_Assignment 02**". Instructions: Compose three different broken chord accompaniments for the same melody. (Lines 1-2 are the original melody and accompaniment.) You must use the same chords but you may alter the duration of the notes, the order in which they played, use open harmony, etc. Try and come up with some broken chord accompaniments that were not presented in this lesson.

Assignment 3

Compose a melodic period that has a pedal point for the accompaniment in the left hand.

Assignment 4

Compose a bass ostinato, and then compose a melody to go with it.

10. BINARY FORM

COMPOSITIONAL FORM

For the remainder of this course we will be studying compositional form. There are many types of compositional forms. This course will cover those most commonly used.

What is form? Simply put, it is the "structure" of a piece. We are not talking here about the structure of the individual components that make up a piece (such as motifs and phrases), but the larger overall structure of a piece.

Let's continue with the analogy to language that we began in *Music Composition 1*.

LANGUAGE	MUSIC
letters	notes
words	motifs
sentences	phrases
paragraphs	periods (and phrase groups)
chapters	sections

Just as paragraphs make up chapters in a book, so in music, periods (and phrase groups) make up what we call "sections". In shorter pieces a section could be made up of a single period whereas in longer pieces a section could be made up of multiple periods.

THEMATIC DESIGN & HARMONIC STRUCTURE

Before we begin delving into the different types of compositional form it is necessary to take note of the two essential elements to form: **thematic design** and **harmonic structure**. These are the two elements that help to delineate one section of music from another. Basically, a section of music is called a "section" of music either because of the thematic material used or because of the harmonic material used (or both). This will become clearer as we study the different types of binary form.

When analyzing music we denote distinct sections of a piece by labeling the sections using letters of the alphabet. The first section of a piece is always labeled as "A".

Binary form is a two-part form. We label first the section "A" and the second section "B". Binary form was very common during the Baroque period. Often times the sections would be repeated, thus making the form "AABB" rather than "AB".

As previously mentioned the sections are determined by the thematic material or the harmonic material (or both). Often times though, the sections can be easily spotted because they are separated by double bar lines with repeat signs.

BINARY FORM

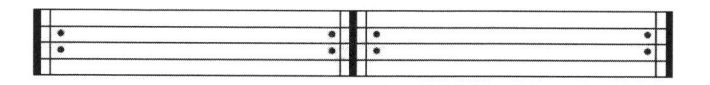

SIMPLE BINARY

Let's begin our study of binary form by looking at how the "thematic" material can delineate a section of music. The most basic way a section of music is termed a "section" is if it has different thematic material. When the "A" and "B" sections each have their own distinct thematic material we call this **simple binary**. Here is a diagram to illustrate this.

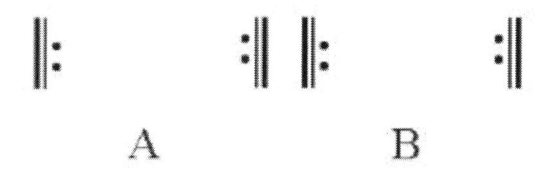

A   B

An example of simple binary would be Beethoven's "Russian Folk Dance". Print the .pdf of the score so that you can study and refer to it. Be sure to listen to the audio as well.

(Lesson 10 - Score 01)

(Lesson 10 - Audio 01)

As you can see, the "A" section and "B" section are separated by double bar lines with repeats. But even without these repeats one could determine the sections of the piece through the thematic material. If you compare measures 1-8 (A section) to measures 9-16 (B section) you will find that there is enough of a difference between the melodic and rhythmic material that each can qualify as its own section. The thematic material in the "A" section begins with 4 eighth notes which rise a 3rd then repeat three times.

The thematic material in the "B" section begins with a quarter note followed by a dotted rhythm which falls downward by 2nds.

As you can see, these two thematic ideas are different both melodically and rhythmically.

It is important to note that the thematic material does not necessarily need to be "entirely" different for a part of the music to be qualified as a unique section. Some of the thematic material can be the same as long as some of it is different. For example, one of the motifs used in the "B" section (measure 10: "F-E-E") is actually borrowed from a motif used in the "A" section (measure 4: "C-B-B"). Take time to recall the principle of unity and variety that we studied in *Music Composition 1*. This is a great example of that principle.

ROUNDED BINARY

The next type of binary form we will be looking at is called **rounded binary**. Like simple binary, it also has two sections. The difference in rounded binary is that thematic material from the "A" section is tacked on to the end of the "B" section. This "rounds" it out so that the piece begins and ends with thematic material from the "A" section. Here is a diagram to illustrate this.

$$\|: a \quad :\| \|: b \quad a :\|$$
$$\quad\; A \qquad\qquad B$$

The upper case letters refer to the sections while the lower case letters refer to the thematic material. For example, the lower case "a" refers to the "a" theme (the motifs) used in the "A" section. The lower case "b" refers to the "b" theme (the motifs) used in the "B" section. The "b" theme is sometimes referred to as the **digression**. This portion of the "B" section is usually very short and cannot stand on its own. The "a" theme then returns usually half way through the "B" section and rounds out the piece. (Typically it is only the 2nd half of "a" that returns and not the "a" theme in its entirety.)

MUSIC COMPOSITION 2

An example of simple binary is "Minuet" by Leopold Mozart. Print the .pdf of the score so that you can study and refer to it. Be sure to listen to the audio as well.

(Lesson 10 - Score 02)

(Lesson 10 - Audio 02)

Measures 1-9 (A section) are made up of the following thematic material which is part of the "a" theme.

Measures 9-12 (1st half of the B section) are made up of the following thematic material which makes up the "b" theme.

Measures 13-16 are the return of the "a" theme. Again, typically it is only the 2nd half of the "a" theme that returns and not "a" theme in its entirety. Here measures 13-16 are a repeat of measures 5-8.

SECTIONAL BINARY

We learned at the beginning of this lesson that there were two elements that delineate one section of music from another: thematic design and harmonic structure. We have seen how thematic design contributes to the form of a piece in both simple binary and rounded binary. We will now look at how harmonic structure contributes to the form of a piece.

If the "A" section ends in the tonic key it is considered "harmonically complete". When the "A" section is harmonically complete we call the form **sectional binary**. Typically this is accomplished through an authentic cadence (or sometimes a plagal cadence).

An example of sectional binary is "Bourrée" by Christoph Graupner. Print the .pdf of the score so that you can study and refer to it. Be sure to listen to the audio as well.

(Lesson 10 - Score 03)

(Lesson 10 - Audio 03)

Lines 1-2 (A section) are in the key of "E minor" and end with an authentic cadence in the last 2 measures of line 2. (V^7 to I or B^7 to Em). Because the "A" section ends in the tonic key it is harmonically complete and the piece is therefore called sectional binary. It does not matter what comes next harmonically in the "B" section as long as the "A" section ends in the tonic key.

Although what comes next in the "B" section does not determine whether the piece is sectional or not, here are some typical harmonic structures of sectional binary form.

When the "A" section is in a major key, the "B" section will typically begin in the dominant key (V) before modulating back to the tonic key (I) at the end. (Important: the Roman numerals in the diagrams refer to the "key" at that point in the piece and not the chord names.)

$$\|: \text{I} \quad :\| \quad \|: \text{V} \quad \text{I} :\|$$

When the "A" section is in a minor key, the "B" section will typically begin in the relative major key (III) before modulating back to the tonic key (i) at the end.

$$\|: \text{i} \quad :\| \quad \|: \text{III} \quad \text{i} :\|$$

"Bourrée" by Christoph Graupner follows the harmonic structure of the preceding diagram. Line 3 (the B section) begins in the relative major (G major) by way of a "V of III" ("D Major" is the "V" chord in the key of "G major", whereas "G major" is the "III" chord as it relates to the original key of "E minor" in the "A" section).

Notice how the thematic material is mostly the same in both sections. In this example, it is not the thematic design that determines the sections, but rather the harmonic structure.

CONTINUOUS BINARY

In sectional binary, the "A" section must end in the tonic key. When the "A" section ends on anything other than the tonic, we call this **continuous binary**. Because the "A" section does not end on the tonic key it is not harmonically complete. It will "continue" on into the "B" section. Here are some typical harmonic structures of continuous binary form.

When the "A" section is in a major key, it will typically modulate to the dominant key (V) at the end of the "A" section. The "B" section will begin in the dominant key (V) before modulating back to the tonic key (I).

$$\|: I \quad V :\| \|: V \quad I :\|$$

When the "A" section is in a minor key, it will typically modulate to the relative major key (III) at the end of the "A" section. The "B" section will begin in the relative major key (III) before modulating back to the tonic key (i).

$$\|: i \quad III :\| \|: III \quad i :\|$$

An example of continuous binary is "Minuet in C" by W. A. Mozart. Print the .pdf of the score so that you can study and refer to it. Be sure to listen to the audio as well.

MUSIC COMPOSITION 2

(Lesson 10 - Score 04)

(Lesson 10 - Audio 04)

Lines 1-2 (A section) begin in the key of C major (I or tonic) and end in the key of G major (V or dominant).

Lines 3-4 (B section) begin in the key of G major (V or dominant) and end in the key of C major (I or tonic).

Once again, notice how the thematic material is mostly the same in both sections. In this example, it is not the thematic design that determines the sections, but rather the harmonic structure.

OTHER BINARY FORMS

The four types of binary form we have studied thus far are: simple binary, rounded binary, sectional binary and continuous binary. Simple and rounded are determined by thematic design while sectional and continuous are determined by harmonic structure. It is important to note that because melody and harmony do no happen in isolation these forms usually occur in combinations. There are four possible combinations.

- Simple Sectional
- Simple Continuous
- Rounded Sectional
- Rounded Continuous

BINARY FORM

Two other terms you should know are **symmetrical**, and **asymmetrical**.

- When the "A" section and the "B" section are the same length we call it "symmetrical" binary.
- When the "A" section and the "B" section are not the same length we call it "asymmetrical" binary. (Typically it is the "B" section that is longer in these instances.)

Memory Questions

What is form?
Form is the overall structure of a piece of music.

What are the two essential elements of form?
The two essential elements of form are thematic design and harmonic structure.

What do thematic design and harmonic structure delineate?
Thematic design and harmonic structure delineate the sections in a piece of music.

What does a section consist of?
A section consists of one or more periods.

How do we label the different sections of a piece?
The different sections of a piece are labeled using the letters of the alphabet.

What is binary form?
Binary form is a form consisting of two sections labeled "A" and "B".

Which types of binary are determined by thematic design?
Simple binary and rounded binary are determined by thematic design.

What is simple binary?
Simple binary is a binary form in which each section has its own distinct thematic material.

What is rounded binary?
Rounded binary is a binary form in which the thematic material from the "A" section is heard again at the tail end of the "B" section.

Which types of binary are determined by harmonic structure?
Sectional binary and continuous binary are determined by harmonic structure.

What is sectional binary?
Sectional binary is a binary form in which the "A" section is harmonically complete.

What does it mean for a section to be harmonically complete?
A section is harmonically complete if it ends in the tonic key.

What is continuous binary?
Continuous binary is a binary form in which the "A" section is harmonically incomplete.

What does it mean for a section to be harmonically incomplete?
A section is harmonically incomplete if it does not end in the

tonic key.

What is symmetrical binary?
Symmetrical binary is a binary form in which the "A" section and the "B" section are the same length.

What is asymmetrical binary?
Asymmetrical binary is a binary form in which the "A" section and the "B" section are different lengths.

Lesson 10 Quiz

Log in to your course at www.udemy.com and take the quiz for this lesson.

IMPORTANT: print the .pdf "German Dance_Beethoven" under the downloadable materials tab before taking the quiz. You will have to answer questions about the music.

Listening Assignments

Sergei Prokofiev (1891 - 1953)
- Lieutenant Kijé, Op. 60 (suite for orchestra)
- Peter and the Wolf (narrator and orchestra)

Igor Stravinsky 1882 - 1971)

- The Firebird (1919 version)

Composition Assignments

Assignment 1

Compose a piece for piano in simple binary form. You may choose the key and meter. Notate the piece using NotePad (or other notation software).

Assignment 2

Compose a piece for piano in rounded binary form. You may choose the key and meter. Notate the piece using NotePad (or other notation software).

Assignment 3

Compose a piece for piano in sectional binary form. You may choose the key and meter. Notate the piece using NotePad (or other notation software).

Assignment 4

Compose a piece for piano in continuous binary form. You may choose the key and meter. Notate the piece using NotePad (or other notation software).

11. TERNARY FORM

SIMPLE TERNARY

The next type of musical form we are going to be studying is **ternary form**. Ternary means "three-part" form. The three sections are labeled "A", "B" and "A". Each section typically ends in an authentic cadence and consists of contrasting thematic material. In ternary form, the sections do not normally repeat as they do in binary form. Here is a diagram that illustrates ternary form.

| A | B | A ||

The "B" section of a piece in ternary form is usually in a key that is related to the key of the "A" section. Most common are the dominant key, the relative major or relative minor key, and the parallel major or parallel minor key. The "B" section and "A" section are typically very contrasting. Ways in which "B" can be contrasting to "A" include, but are not limited to: contrasting key, contrasting tempo, contrasting dynamics, contrasting rhythmic and melodic material, etc. When "A" returns but is slightly varied we label the form as "ABA¹".

Note: Ternary forms can also include "transitions" between each section and a "coda". These terms will be explained momentarily.

Ternary form was used in the 17th and early 18th centuries in opera arias. The form was called the "da capo aria" because the final "A" section was not written out. Instead of writing out the entire "A" section a second time, the words "da capo" ("from the head" or "from the beginning") told the performer to replay the original "A" section note for note.

In the 18th century, the minuet and trio was written using ternary form. (Minuet - Trio - Minuet). Ternary form was also used in single movement of larger pieces such as string quartets, symphonies, and sonatas.

In the 19th century ternary form was used in short piano pieces. An example of simple ternary written in the 19th century is "Ballade" by Johann Friedrich Burgmüller. Print the .pdf of the score so that you can study and refer to it. Be sure to listen to the audio as well.

(Lesson 11 - Score 01)

(Lesson 11 - Audio 01)

Measures 1-30 (A section): The piece begins in the key of "C minor". It is characterized by the mysterious sounding 16th note pattern and staccato eighth notes. A transition from the "A" section to the "B" section occurs in measures 24-30 (one could also argue that it occurs in measures 19-30). A transition is basically a portion of music that helps the composer shift from one section of a piece to another (or from one theme to another). It can be made up of thematic material from the "A" section, thematic material from the "B" section (in this case it foreshadows what is to come), or it can be completely different material.

Measures 31-56 (B section): The thematic material in this section contrasts nicely with the thematic material from the "A" section. Both the rhythmic and melodic material is different, as well as the overall mood (mysteriously vs. sweetly). Harmonically the "B" section is distinguished from the "A" section due to the difference in key. The "B" section is in the key of "C major" (the parallel key to the key of "C minor"). Measures 47-56 is a transition back to the "A" section. It uses thematic material from the "B" section.

Measures 57-86 (A section): We can see here that the "A" section returns almost entirely note for note. It is basically a complete restatement of "A". The composer could have chosen to restate "A" in a slightly varied way, in which case it would be labeled as "A^1".

Measures 87-96 (Coda): After the second "A" section we find ten extra measures that have been tacked on to the end of the piece. The thematic material used here is most definitely taken from the "A" section. (The composer could have used thematic material from the "A" section, "B" section, transitions, a combination of these, or completely new material) This "extra" part that is added on is called the "coda". Coda is Italian for "tail". Think of it as a final statement that in a sense sums up the whole piece.

TERNARY VS. ROUNDED BINARY

At this point you may be wondering what the difference is between ternary form and rounded binary form. If you recall from the last lesson, the "A" section of rounded binary contains the "a" theme. The "B" section of rounded binary contains the "b" theme (the digression) followed by a return to the "a" theme about half way through the "B" section. The "a, b, a" looks similar to ternary form but it is not.

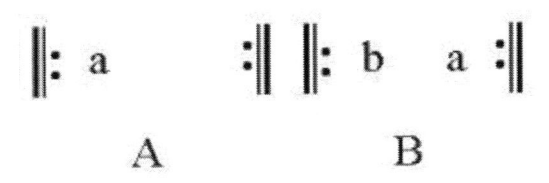

$$\|{:}\ a\ {:}\|\ \|{:}\ b\quad a\ {:}\|$$

$$\ \ \ \ \ \ A\qquad\qquad B$$

Ternary form is different from rounded binary in a few distinct ways.

1. The "B" section in ternary is much longer than the "b" theme in the "B" section of rounded binary.
2. The "B" section is an independent section that would make sense if played on its own, whereas the "b" theme in the "B" section of rounded binary would not make sense if played on its own.
3. The "B" section in ternary is typically very contrasting to "A" whereas the "b" theme in the "B" section of rounded binary is usually more closely related to "a".

TERNARY FORM

COUMPOUND TERNARY

Sometimes a composer will write a piece of music that consists of a form within a form. For example, the three sections of a ternary piece could each be made up of a binary form. We call this **compound ternary**. Here is a diagram to illustrate.

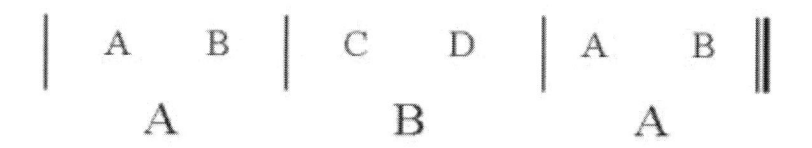

```
| A    B  |  C    D  |  A    B ||
     A          B          A
```

As you can see, the overall structure is ternary (the larger font). The first "A" section of the ternary form is made up of a smaller binary form labeled "A" and "B". The "B" section of the ternary form is also made up of a smaller binary form labeled "C" and "D". The final "A" section of the ternary form is again made up of a smaller binary form labeled "A" and "B".

An example of compound ternary is the 5th movement of Bach's "Cello Suite in G". Print the .pdf of the score so that you can study and refer to it. Be sure to listen to the audio as well.

(Lesson 11 - Score 02)

(Lesson 11 - Audio 02)

Minuet 1 is the "A" section of the overall ternary form. It is made up of a binary form where measures 1-8 are the "A" section and measures 9-24 are the "B" section. Both of these sections repeat.

Minuet 2 is the "B" section of the overall ternary form. It is made up of a binary form where measures 25-32 are the "A" section and measures 33-48 are the "B" section. Both of these sections repeat.

Minuet 1 is then played again without repeats for the final "A" section of the overall ternary form.

Now that we've looked at one possible structuring of compound ternary (multiple binary forms within a ternary form), let's take a look at another possible structuring: multiple ternary forms within a ternary form. Here is a diagram to help illustrate this.

$$\| A\ B\ A\ |\ C\ D\ C\ |\ A\ B\ A \|$$
$$A \qquad\qquad B \qquad\qquad A$$

As you can see, section "A" has a ternary form within itself, section "B" has a ternary form within itself, and the final section "A" also has a ternary form within itself. This type of compound ternary is also sometimes referred to as "complex" ternary. This is to distinguish it from compound ternary which is made up of multiple binary forms.

Composers have used many other combinations of binary and ternary forms. Here are some examples.

ABA | CD | ABA
A B A

(ternary compounded of two ternary forms and one binary form)

TERNARY FORM

AB | CDC | AB
A   B   A

(ternary compounded of two binary forms and one ternary form)

ABA | CDC
A   B

(binary compounded of two ternary forms)

Memory Questions

What is ternary form?
Ternary form is a form consisting of three sections labeled "A", "B" and "A".

What type of cadence does each section in ternary form typically end with?
Each section in ternary form typically ends with an authentic cadence.

Is the thematic material in the "A" and "B" sections of ternary form usually similar or contrasting?
The thematic material in the "A" and "B" sections of ternary form is usually contrasting.

How does the "B" section in ternary form differ from the "b" theme in the "B" section of rounded binary?
The "B" section in ternary from is longer, independent, and contrasting.

What is compound ternary?
Compound ternary is a type of ternary form in which each section is made up of smaller binary forms.

What is complex ternary?
Complex ternary is a type of ternary form in which each section is made up of smaller ternary forms.

Lesson 11 Quiz

Log in to your course at www.udemy.com and take the quiz for this lesson.

IMPORTANT: print the .pdf "Wild Rider_Schumann" under the downloadable materials tab before taking the quiz. You will have to answer questions about the music.

Listening Assignments

Carl Orff (1895 - 1982)

- Carmina Burana

Composition Assignments

Assignment 1

Compose a piece for piano in simple ternary form. You may choose the key and meter. Notate the piece using NotePad (or other notation software).

12. RONDO & ARCH FORMS

FIVE-PART FORM

The next form we are going to look at is called **rondo form**. Rondo form consists of a principle section which reappears periodically between other contrasting sections. The most common form of rondo consists of five sections, thus rondo form is sometimes called "five-part form". The sections are labeled as follows.

$$\|\,A\,|\,B\,|\,A\,|\,C\,|\,A\,\|$$

Rondo form is all about departure and return; departure from the principle theme and then return to the principle theme. The principle section is referred to as the "refrain". The contrasting sections are referred to as "episodes". In five-part rondo form, "A" is the refrain, and "B" and "C" are the episodes. The refrain thus supplies us with the element of unity, while the episodes supply us with the element of variety.

The "A" section of a rondo is usually made up of a rounded binary form (lesson 10). The episodes will typically be in a contrasting but related key to the "A section" (dominant or relative key). They will also use contrasting thematic material.

The name "rondo" and its basic structure may have its origins in a medieval form of poetry called "rondeau". This poetic form consisted of couplets that reappeared periodically between longer poetical sections. During the classical period the rondo was used both as a single movement in larger works (sonatas, serenades, and concertos) and also as a form for an individual piece (shorter piano solos). Fewer examples exist in the music of the late 19th century and the 20th century, as the form was used less frequently.

The most famous example of five-part rondo form is "Für Elise" by Beethoven. Print the .pdf of the score so that you can study and refer to it. Be sure to listen to the audio as well.

(Lesson 12 - Score 01)

(Lesson 12 - Audio 01)

Measures 1-23 (A section): The refrain is in the key of "A minor". If you study it closely you will notice that it is made up of a rounded binary form. The last three chords of measure 23 are a sort of very brief transition to the first episode "B". They are the "V" of the key of "F major" followed by the "I" and again by the "V". This helps to establish the new key in the next section.

Measures 24-38 (B section): This first episode is very light and joyous which contrasts nicely with the bitter sweet sounds heard in the refrain (A section). It begins in the key of "F major". A modulation to "C major" begins in measure 29 and by measure 31 we are in the key of "C major" for a secondary theme (consisting of 32nd notes) up until 34. Measures 35-38 are transitional material (taken from the "A" section) that shifts us back into the key of "A minor" and the return of the refrain at the end of measure 38 (last 2 notes).

Measures 38-59 (A section): This is the refrain heard for the second time.

Measures 60-82 (C section): The second episode is in the same key as the refrain ("A minor"). It is very dark and ominous which contrasts nicely with the other previously heard sections. It consists of a driving 16th note bass pattern. Measure 78 begins the "re-transition" into the return of the final "A" section. (In a rondo, the term "re-transition" refers to a transition which is used to move from an episode back to the refrain.)

Measures 83-end (A section): This is the refrain heard for the final time.

SEVEN-PART FORM

When a rondo contains 3 episodes (B, C, and D) it is in seven-part form.

‖ A | B | A | C | A | D | A ‖

In the late 18th and early 19th centuries the "D" section would often times be replaced by a second "B" section which was played in the original tonic key.

$$|\ A\ |\ B\ |\ A\ |\ C\ |\ A\ |\ B^1\ |\ A\ \|$$

Here is the typical harmonic structure of a seven-part rondo during this time period.

<u>If written in a major key:</u>

- All "A" sections were in the tonic key (I)
- The first "B" section was typically in the dominant key (V)
- The "C" section was typically in the subdominant key (IV), relative minor (vi), or parallel minor (i).
- The second "B" section was in the tonic key (I)

<u>If written in a minor key:</u>

- All "A" sections were in the tonic key (i)
- The first "B" section was typically in the dominant key (V), or relative major (III).
- The "C" section was typically in the subdominant key (iv), or submediant key (VI).
- The second "B" section was in the tonic key (i)

For an example of a seven-part rondo, listen to "Viennese Music Clock" from the *Háry János Suite* by Zoltán Kodály. Due to copyright restrictions some of the pieces used in the examples in this course do not have downloadable audio. To find a recording, check on-line sources such as www.musopen.org, obtain a subscription to www.naxos.com, or check your local library. Your library may also subscribe to www.freegalmusic.com. If they do, you can download a specific amount of music each week for free and its yours to keep.

ARCH FORM

Another five-part form is **arch form**. Unlike the rondo forms, arch form does not consist of a principle section which reappears periodically between other contrasting sections. In arch form each section is heard in sequential order (A, B, C). The piece is then worked backwards so that the "A" and "B" sections return in reverse order. Think of arch form as walking forward and then retracing your steps backwards. Here is a diagram illustrating arch form.

$$\| A \mid B \mid C \mid B \mid A \|$$

For an example of a song written in arch form, listen to the 1st movement of the *English Folk Song Suite* by Ralph Vaughan Williams titled "March: Seventeen Come Sunday". Each section is based on a different folk song. The "A" section features the folk song "Seventeen Come Sunday, the "B" section features the folk song

"Pretty Caroline", and the "C" section features the Christmas carol "Dives and Lazarus". Find a recording of the 1st movement and see if you can identify each section.

Note: As with most forms, the return of any section does not necessarily have to be an exact "note for note" copy of the first instance of the section; there can exist some degree of variation if the composer so desires.

Memory Questions

What is rondo form?
Rondo form is a form consisting of a principle section which reappears periodically between other contrasting sections.

How many sections does rondo form typically have?
Rondo form typically has either five sections or seven sections.

How are the sections in five-part rondo form labeled?
The sections in five-part rondo form are labeled "ABACA".

How are the sections in seven-part rondo form labeled?
The sections in seven-part rondo form are labeled "ABACADA".

How was the seven-part rondo labeled in the late 18th and early 19th centuries?
In the late 18th and early 19th centuries the seven-part rondo was labeled "ABACAB^{1}A", with the second "B" section being played in the original tonic key.

What is the principle section in a rondo called?
The principle section in a rondo is called the refrain.

What are the contrasting sections in a rondo called?
The contrasting sections in a rondo are called episodes.

What is arch form?
Arch form is a five-part form in which each section is heard in sequential order before being worked backwards so that the "A" and "B" sections return in reverse order.

How are the sections in arch form labeled?
The sections in arch form are labeled "ABCBA".

Lesson 12 Quiz

Log in to your course at www.udemy.com and take the quiz for this lesson.

IMPORTANT: print the .pdf "Sonata Pathetique_Beethoven" under the downloadable materials tab before taking the quiz. You will have to answer questions about the music.

Listening Assignments

George Gershwin (1898 - 1937)

- Rhapsody in Blue
- "Summertime" from the opera "Porgy and Bess"

Aaron Copland (1900 - 1990)

- Fanfare for the Common Man
- "Hoe-Down" from "Four Dance Episodes from Rodeo"

Composition Assignments

Assignment 1

Compose a piece for piano in rondo form. You may choose the key and meter. Notate the piece using NotePad (or other notation software).

13. STROPHIC & VARIATION FORMS

ONE-PART FORM

The next compositional form we are going to look at is the **strophic** (STROH-fik) **form**. This form is primarily used in music with lyrics which are sung in verses, such as folk songs and hymns (although instrumental pieces can be written using strophic form as well). A piece written in strophic form will therefore be a repetition of the same bit of music over and over, while only the words change with each verse. Two well-known examples of strophic form are "Silent Night", and "Amazing Grace".

Strophic form is sometimes called "one-part form" since it has only one section. Since strophic form consists of only one section repeated over and over, it would be labeled using only the letter "A". For example, a piece with 3 verses would be labeled "AAA", while a piece with 4 verses would be labeled "AAAA".

A form that is in a sense the opposite of strophic form is **through-composed.** Through-composed music is music that is "non-repeating". Rather than one section repeating (AAAAA...) each section is completely different (ABCDE…). In songs with words this means that each verse has its own unique melody. For an example of a through-composed piece, listen to "Der Erlkönig" by Franz Schubert.

Note: Through-composed can also refer to music that is "non-sectional", that is, music that does not really have definable sections and is a continuous flow of music.

THEME AND VARIATIONS

The next two forms we are going to look at are types of **variation form**. Some music theorists classify variation form as a type of strophic form since these pieces consist of variations of a single section. The first is called **theme and variations**. This form consists of a main theme followed by variations of the theme. Since the piece is one section repeated with variations, the music is labeled as "A^1, A^2, A^3, etc."

The theme and variations form has been a popular form since the 16th century. The theme can be varied in many different ways, which include but are not limited to a change in rhythmic structure, melodic structure, harmonic structure, dynamics, tempo, and key. Up until the end of the 18th century, the variations composers made were still easily recognizable as a variation of the original theme. As time went on variations became more and more elaborate and so ornate that the original theme was much harder to hear in the variations. Today the theme and variation structure can be found in a lot of jazz music.

For an example of a piece written in theme and variations form, listen to "Caprice No. 24 in A minor" for violin by Niccolò Paganini.

MUSIC COMPOSITION 2

See if you can hear the theme followed by 11 variations and a finale.

(Lesson 13 - Score 01)

For another example of a piece written in theme and variations form, listen to "Variations on a Theme of Corelli" by Sergei Rachmaninoff. It consists of a theme followed by 20 variations. There is an intermezzo (a brief interlude) between variations 13 and 14 and a Coda after variation 20.

(Lesson 13 - Score 02)

CHACONNE

Another type of variation form is the **chaconne** (shä-ˈkȯn). A chaconne is a set of variations based on a short repeating harmonic progression, very frequently on a short repeating bass line. This harmonic progression or repeating base line is the foundation of the entire piece and is the tool by which variations can be carried out. They were very popular in the Baroque period and were typically in 3/4 meter.

For an example of a chaconne, listen to the "Chaconne in F minor" by Johann Pachelbel. Here is the short repeating bass line on which the harmonic progression and the entire piece are based.

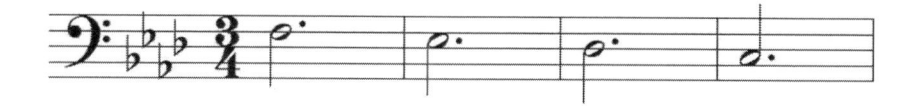

STROPHIC & VARIATION FORMS

(Lesson 13 - Score 03)

For another example of chaconne form, listen to Pachelbel's "Canon in D". This is probably the most famous and recognizable piece which incorporates the chaconne form (it is actually a mixture of chaconne, and canonic material). Here is the short repeating bass line on which the harmonic progression and the entire piece are based.

(Lesson 13 - Score 04)

Memory Questions

What is strophic form?
Strophic form is a form consisting of one section that is repeated.

Where is strophic form primarily used?
Strophic form is primarily used in music with lyrics which are sung in verses, such as folk songs and hymns.

What is through-composed music?
Through-composed music is music that is "non-repeating"; each section is completely different.

What are two types of variation form?
Two types of variation form are theme and variations, and chaconne.

What is theme and variations form?
Theme and variations form consists of a main theme followed by multiple variations of the theme.

What is a chaconne?
A chaconne is a set of variations based on a short repeating harmonic progression, very frequently on a short repeating bass line.

Lesson 13 Quiz

Log in to your course at www.udemy.com and take the quiz for this lesson.

Listening Assignments

Dmitri Shostakovich (1906 - 1975)

- Piano Concerto No. 2 in F Major

Samuel Barber (1910 - 1981)

- Adagio for Strings

Composition Assignments

Assignment 1

Log into your course at www.udemy.com. You will find the assignments for this lesson in section 13 under the "Downloadable Materials" tab. Print the .pdf file "**Lesson 13_Assignment 01**". Instructions: Compose a chaconne in the key of "A minor" for piano using the bass line provided for you. Write between 8-12 variations based on this repeating bass line. Focus primarily on variations in the rhythmic and melodic structure of the right hand. Notate using NotePad (or other notation software).

14. SONATA FORM

1ST MOVMENT FORM

One of the most significant and influential forms of the classical period was the **sonata form**. A sonata is a larger scale instrumental piece, originating from the 16th century, consisting of multiple movements (usually 2-4). Each movement of the sonata was written in a different form. For example, the 2nd movement was typically in ternary form, while the 3rd or final movement was typically in rondo form. The term "sonata form" refers to the form that the 1st movement was typically written in. This is why sonata form is also known as "1st movement form". (Although it should be noted that sonata form was occasionally used as a 2nd or 3rd movement, or as a finale.) Sonata form is also sometimes referred to as "sonata-allegro form" since the 1st movement of a sonata was typically played at a quick tempo (allegro). The form itself began to take shape and become solidified during the classical period primarily through the works of Mozart, Haydn and Beethoven.

SONATA FORM

The following diagram will help illustrate sonata form. There are three sections: the **exposition, development** and **recapitulation**. We will take a look at each one in turn. Note that the diagram shows the typical harmonic structure of the form when written in a major key and when written in a minor key.

	‖: Exposition :‖	‖: Development	Recapitulation :‖	
	primary secondary theme theme	develop one or both themes or add new material	primary theme	secondary theme
major key:	(I) (V)	(V and lots of modulating)	(I)	(I)
minor key:	(i) (III or V)	(III or V and lots of modulating)	(i)	(i)

The exposition is the section in which the themes are introduced (or "exposed") to the listener. In the exposition there is a primary theme and a secondary theme. The primary theme is in the tonic while the secondary theme is in a related key. There is usually a transition between the primary and secondary themes that assists in the modulation to the new key. After the secondary theme is heard there may be a codetta (small tail) which solidifies the modulation to the new key typically with an authentic cadence.

The development section is the place where the composer is free to expand upon, and further "develop", any of the themes used in the exposition. This section can also contain completely new thematic material. Typically the development section is in the new key in which the exposition section ended (although it can be in a related key). Often during this section there is a lot of modulating through different keys. Development is done primarily through manipulation of the thematic material and key changes. The development section typically feels unstable and is in stark contrast to the sections before and after it. The length of the development was typically shorter than the exposition during the classical period and longer than the exposition during the romantic period. There is usually a re-transition between the development and recapitulation to assist in the modulation back to the original key of the piece.

The recapitulation is basically a "recap" of the exposition. Typically the only difference is that the secondary theme is in the tonic key this time around (although there may be other slight variations). A "coda" is sometimes added on to the end of the recapitulation.

Now that we have the basic structure of sonata form laid out, let's look at the 1st movement of a piece written in sonata form. The title of this piece is "Sonatina in C major" by Muzio Clementi. A "sonatina" is basically a short sonata. Although we will be looking at a sonatina in this example, the form used is still "sonata form". Print the .pdf of the score so that you can study and refer to it. Be sure to listen to the audio as well.

(Lesson 14 - Score 01)

(Lesson 14 - Audio 01)

Exposition (Measures 1-15): The primary theme is in the tonic key of "C major" and contains the following motif.

There is a very brief transition (last beat of measure 6 through the end of 7) which assists in the modulation to the key of "G major" in measure 8.

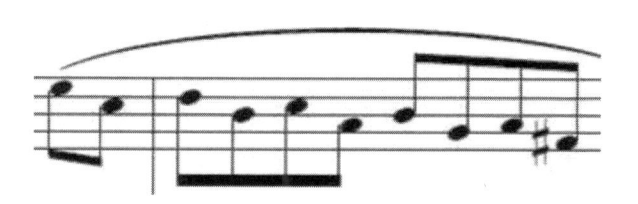

Measure 8 begins the secondary theme in the new key of "G major" and is made up of the following motifs.

A codetta occurs in measures 12-15 ending on an authentic cadence (V to I) which solidifies the new key of "G major".

Development (Measures 16-23): The development begins in the parallel minor (C minor) of the exposition key (C major). The final chord of the exposition (G major) becomes the first chord (dominant chord) of the development section. This is how the composer is able to get to "C minor". "G" also serves as the dominant to "C major" and is used in measure 23 to re-transition back to the original tonic key.

The thematic material the composer has chosen to further develop in this section is the primary theme and the transition theme from the exposition section. The primary theme is seen first as part of the dominant chord and then a "C minor" chord.

The transition theme from the exposition is seen once again in measure 18 (right hand), this time in the minor key and using quarter notes rather than eighth notes.

It can also be found hidden in every other note (accented notes) of the left hand in measures 20-21.

SONATA FORM

Recapitulation (Measures 24-38):

In this particular piece the "recap" is not an exact copy of the exposition. There are a few slight alterations. The primary theme is transposed an octave lower (measures 24-27). The primary theme is seen again in measure 28 with the intervals of the chord moving in the opposite direction, and again in measure 29 using a different inversion of the chord. Since the secondary theme in the recapitulation is always in the tonic, no modulation is necessary in the transition (measure 30). Measure 31 begins the secondary theme in the tonic key of "C major". The codetta reoccurs slightly altered (measures 35-38) and ends with an authentic cadence to solidify the return to the home key.

This lesson concludes *Music Composition 2* and our study of harmonic composition and compositional form. For your final assignment you will be asked to compose a one movement piano piece written in sonata form. You may obtain a professional recording of any of the pieces you composed for the assignments in this course for a fee. If you are interested please contact the author at his web site: www.ComposerJonathanPeters.com

Memory Questions

What is a sonata?
A sonata is a larger scale instrumental piece, originating from the 16th century, consisting of multiple movements, the first of which was typically written in sonata form.

What is sonata form?
Sonata form consists of three sections in the following order: the exposition, development and recapitulation.

What is the exposition?
The exposition is the section in which the themes are introduced to the listener.

How many themes does the exposition section typically contain?
The exposition section typically contains a primary theme and a secondary theme.

What is the development section?
The development section is the place where the composer is free to expand upon, and further develop, any of the themes used in the exposition.

What is the recapitulation?
The recapitulation is a restatement of the exposition section with the secondary theme in the tonic key.

SONATA FORM

Lesson 14 Quiz

Log in to your course at www.udemy.com and take the quiz for this lesson.

IMPORTANT: print the .pdf "Sonatina_Diabelli" under the downloadable materials tab before taking the quiz. You will have to answer questions about the music.

Listening Assignments

Benjamin Britten (1913 - 1976)

- Simple Symphony, Op. 4
- The Young Person's Guide to the Orchestra

Leonard Bernstein (1918 - 1990)

- Overture to the opera "Candide"

Composition Assignments

Assignment 1

Compose a one movement piano piece written in sonata form. You may choose the meter and key. Follow the basic structure laid out in this lesson. You may include transitions, re-transitions, codetta and coda if you wish. Notate using NotePad (or other notation software).

INDEX

A

Accompaniment
  alberti bass, 94–95
  block chord, 92–94
  broken chord, 94–97
  ostinato, 100–101
  pedal point, 100
  waltz, 96
Alberti Bass, 94–95
Arch Form, 132–33
Authentic Cadence, 43, 46, 50–52, 111, 119

B

Binary
  assymetrical, 115
  continuous, 113–14
  other, 114, 125
  rounded, 109–10
  sectional, 111–12
  simple, 107–9
  symmetrical, 115
Block Chord Accompaniment, 92–94
Broken Chord Accompaniment, 94–97

C

Cadences, 43
Chaconne, 138–39
Chord Changes
  stark, 26–27
  strong, 26
  subtle, 26

Chord Progressions
  basic structure, 3–7, 21–24
  circle progressions, 38–39
  devloping, 32–39
  extending, 32–35
  partial progressions, 37–38
  progression chains, 35–36
Chords
  altered, 62–67
  borrowed, 59–62
  chromatic, 59, 62
  diatonic, 2
  pivot, 72–75
  primary, 3, 6
  secondary, 18–20
  secondary dominant, 62–67, 75–76
  similarity between, 25–27
Coda, 121
Codetta, 143

D

Deceptive Cadence, 43, 45
Development Section, 143–44
Dominant Function, 6

E

Exposition Section, 143

F

Form
  arch, 132–33
  binary, 105–15
  chaconne, 138–39
  definition, 105
  rondo, 128–32

sonata, 142–47
strophic, 136
ternary, 119–25
theme and variation, 137–38
through-composed, 136–37
variation, 137–39

Function, 6–7, 18–24, 32–35, 37, 44–46, 59–60, 63–64, 66
definition, 6
dominant, 6
extending the, 32–35
pre-dominant, 6
substitutes, 19–24
tonic, 6

H

Half Cadence, 43–44, 50–52
Harmonic Period, 50–55
Harmonic Phrase, 43–46
answer phrase, 50–52, 54
antecedent phrase, 50–52, 54
consequent phrase, 50–52, 54
question phrase, 50–52, 54
types of, 44
Harmonic Rhythm, 83–88
Harmonic Structure, 111–14
Homophonic, 91–97
Homorhythmic, 97–98

M

Modulation
altered chord, 75–76
direct, 79
pivot-chord, 72–75
pivot-tone, 77
sequential, 78
Musical Texture. *See* Texture

N

Notation Software, 12

O

Ostinato, 100–101

P

Pedal Point, 100
Period, 50–52
contrasting, 52
double period, 54–55
parallel, 52
parallel double, 55
three-phrase, 52–53
Phrase Group, 52–53
Picardy Third, 62
Pivot-tone, 77
Plagal Cadence, 43, 75, 111
Polyphonic, 98–99
Pre-dominant Function, 6

R

Recapitulation Section, 144
Re-transition, 130, 144
Rondo
five-part, 128–30
seven-part, 130–32

S

Secondary Dominants, 62–67, 75–76
Section, 105–6
Sonata Form
coda, 144

codetta, 143
development, 143–44
exposition, 143
primary theme, 143
recapitulation, 144
re-transition, 144
secondary theme, 143
transition, 143

Strophic Form, 136

Substitution Chords
chromatic, 59–67
diatonic, 18–24

T

Ternary
complex, 124
compound, 123–24
other, 124–25
simple, 119–21
vs. rounded binary, 122

Texture, 91–101
homophonic, 91–97
homorhythmic, 97–98
polyphonic, 98–99

Thematic Design, 106, 111–12, 106–12, 114

Theme and Variation Form, 137–38

Through-composed, 136–37

Tonic Function, 6

Tonicization, 63, 73

Transition, 121, 143

V

Variation Form, 137–39

Voice Leading, 7–9

W

Waltz Accompaniment, 96

ABOUT THE AUTHOR

Jonathan Peters is an award-winning composer currently residing in the beautiful state of Colorado. He has worked in the music business for 24 years as teacher, director, composer, and recording artist. Mr. Peters holds a B.A. in liberal arts from Thomas Aquinas College and continued his graduate work at California State University Northridge where he studied advanced composition, theory, orchestration, and film scoring.

Composer and Recording Artist

Mr. Peters has completed over 40 works including 2 full length operas, a symphony, orchestral works, chamber music, choral pieces, and works for solo piano. His pieces have won many awards and recognitions including 1st place in the 1996 Composers Today Contest. He has professionally recorded and produced 6 CDs. His music has been performed both in the United States and Europe, is heard on the radio, and sells in over 50 stores world-wide. He is also the author of the *Scholastic Music Series*, a collection of educational CDs that use music as a tool to teach various academic subjects. The series has received starred reviews from *School Library Journal* and is carried in libraries throughout the country.

Teacher and Director

Over the past 24 years Mr. Peters has given lessons in piano, composition, orchestration and music theory. He has worked with various orchestras, has been a guest conductor with the Cypress Pops Orchestra and has also directed various choirs in southern California.

Author

Mr. Peters is the author of three books on music: *Music Theory*, *Music Composition 1*, and *Music Composition 2*.

www.ComposerJonathanPeters.com